Baking Artisan Pastries & Breads

QUARRY

Baking Artisan Pastries & Breads

SWEET AND SAVORY BAKING FOR BREAKFAST, BRUNCH, AND BEYOND

BEVERLY MASSACHUSETTS

QUARRY BOOKS

CIRIL HITZ
FOREWORD BY
PETER REINHART

First published in the United States of America by
Quarry Books, a member of
Quayside Publishing Group
100 Cummings Center
Suite 406-L
Beverly, Massachusetts 01915-6101
Telephone: (978) 282-9590
Fax: (978) 283-2742
www.quarrybooks.com

Library of Congress Cataloging-in-Publication Data

Hitz, Ciril.
  Baking artisan pastries and breads : sweet and savory baking for breakfast, brunch,
and beyond / Ciril Hitz ; photography by Kylee Hunnibell Hitz.
    p. cm.
  ISBN-13: 978-1-59253-564-4
  ISBN-10: 1-59253-564-X
  1. Pastry. 2. Bread. I. Title.
  TX773.H567 2009
  641.8'15--dc22

                                                                2009021088
                                                                CIP

ISBN-13: 978-1-59253-564-4
ISBN-10: 1-59253-564-X

10 9 8 7 6 5 4 3 2 1

Cover Design: Sussner Design Co.
Book layout: Rachel Fitzgibbon, studio rkf
Photography by Kylee Hunnibell Hitz
DVD filmed and produced by Nick Versteeg, DV Cuisine/www.dvcuisine.com
Printed in Singapore

To my wife, Kylee

You are the light that makes me shine.

Contents

Foreword by Peter Reinhart 8
Introduction 10

PART ONE:
Basics 12

Chapter One:
Ingredients 14

Flour 16
Sugars and Sweeteners 18
Fats 21
Leaveners 24
Eggs 28
Flavorings 30

Chapter Two:
Equipment 32

Scales 34
Mixers 34
Ovens 36
Food Processors 37
Baking Forms 37
Other Tools and Equipment 39

Chapter Three:
Techniques 46

Measuring 48
Quick Bread Techniques 50
Rubbing 50
Creaming 52
Blending 53

Yeasted Dough Techniques 54
    Pre-ferments 54
    Mixing 56
    Shaping 62
    Proofing and Retarding 64
    Lamination 64
Time-Saving Techniques 65

PART TWO:

Baking 66

Chapter Four:
Quick Breads, Muffins, and Scones 68

    Cranberry-Orange Scones 70
    Ginger Scones 72
    Savory Scones 74
    Basic Biscuits 76
    Swiss Carrot Cake 78
    Pumpkin Muffins 80
    Southwest Corn Bread 82
    Zucchini Bread 84
    Banana Muffins 86
    Tirolean Chocolate Muffins 88
    Bran Muffins 90
    English Muffins 92
    Mixed-Berry Muffins 94
    Whole Wheat Cinnamon Raisin Bagels 96

Chapter Five:
Enriched Dough 98

    Classic Brioche 100
    Lemon Brioche Doughnuts 102
    Pumpkin Cream Brioche 104
    Rum-Raisin-Almond Brioche 106
    Apple Kuchen 108
    Panettone 110
    Stollen 112
    Gibassier 115
    Bostock 118
    Basic Sweet Dough 120
    Pecan Sticky Buns 122
    Sweet Glazed Cinnamon Buns 124
    Tea Ring 126
    Russian Braid 128

Chapter Six:
Laminated Dough 130

    Laminated Dough Techniques 132
    All-Purpose Danish 136
    Croissants 140
    Whole Wheat Ham and Cheese
       Croissants 142
    Ultimate Chocolate Croissants 144
    Chocolate-Cinnamon Swirls 146

Chapter Seven:
Fillings, Glazes, Toppings, and Spreads 148

Appendix

    Troubleshooting 158
    Charts and Conversions 167
    Resources 168
    Glossary 170
    Index 171
    Acknowledgments 175
    About the Author 176
    About the Photographer 176

This is a great time to be a baker. (The bakery business, however—that's for the few and the brave). The art and craft of baking for the sheer joy of it is enjoying a golden era, worldwide. The home-baking movement is ever-expanding, a subculture full of people hungry for knowledge culled from the professional community. Simultaneously, the professionals are seeking out masters from previous generations, as well as new frontiers of information, to expand their skills. Wonderful new books full of innovative techniques appear every season, feeding this insatiable hunger. This hunger is a passionate yearning for authenticity, beauty, and, above all, exquisite flavor, and it's what interests me the most. Those who feed these hungry people especially intrigue me. The current name for these folks is *artisans*, a term, I fear, that is in danger of dilution through misuse and appropriation by the marketing industry.

My thoughts on the word *artisan* apply to craftsmen in fine woodworking, pottery, glasswork, and other non-food crafts, or who make cheese, fine chocolates, beers and, of course, chefs of all types. But because Ciril Hitz and his books epitomize and embody the proper expression of this term, artisan, I will focus on the world of baking. It is important to note that Ciril could have easily remained an artisan working in the ceramic and furniture-making mediums of his earlier life had he not found his current calling as a baker and baking teacher. People such as Ciril may be the ones to revitalize the term through demonstrating the distinctions between true artisanship and marketing pretense.

The products photographed in these pages embody authenticity—the real deal. Having sat in on Ciril's classes over the years when we worked together at the Providence campus of Johnson & Wales University, and observed his attention to detail and the degree of precision he instills in his students, made me one of his biggest fans. More important was the sense of satisfaction and pride of achievement emanating from his students after their training, as they were introduced to their inherent artisan potential.

Beyond the beauty of artisans' work, another hallmark is their ability to inspire and ignite transformation. I call it *transformation* because it causes a radical change from one thing into something new and different. A craftsperson expresses this act through the medium of his or her craft, but an artisan teacher has to use the craft to initiate a transformation in the student, too. In this sense, a baking teacher's product is not the transformation of flour and leaven into pastries and bread but, rather, the transformation of the students themselves.

I believe that those who embrace the instruction and teachings in these pages also become candidates for the kind of transmission that Ciril's full-time students experience. That is a lot to lay on any book and, knowing the natural humility and humanity of Ciril, he might be uncomfortable with me saying it, but he did, after all, ask me write this foreword with full latitude to speak my mind. So, as one who has watched him teach, and studied his methodology, allow me to give all who dare proceed the following suggestions:

• Follow his instructions, even if you think you know better. I've heard Ciril tell his students, "I know these formulas work because I've thoroughly tested them, but I can only guarantee them if you follow my directions exactly." (To be fair, Ciril also tells them that once they've mastered the procedures they can feel free to improvise and build on what he's taught them.)

• Study the *photos* as well as the written procedures and emulate the care you see demonstrated.

• Study the *procedures* as well as the photos and try to replicate the steps accurately. Don't rush. There is beauty in the process.

• Use his organizational system as a template upon which to model your own baking and cooking. You will soon find yourself working smarter and, eventually, faster.

Traditionally, there has been very little patient, gentle mentoring in the world of baking and pastry chefs. It used to be sink or swim, do or die. The current generation of artisan baking teachers are forging new ground in which patience as well as structure and discipline are a virtue, even an improvement, in passing knowledge from one generation to the next. Because of this, I foresee a reclamation of the term *artisan*, rescued from those who think of it as a mere slogan or way of capitalizing on the groundwork lain by real craftsmen and women. If artisans are, as we see reflected by people like Ciril, the mentors and role models of those who hunger and thirst after the elusive real deal, then we also need a generation of mentees to fortify the term *artisan* and to protect it from dilution. That, fellow readers and users of this book, includes you.

In short, being an artisan is not what someone does but, rather, it's what someone is.

Peter Reinhart
May 2009
Charlotte, North Carolina

There were many reasons I felt compelled to follow up my first book, *Baking Artisan Bread*, with a book on pastries and breads, but two are most prominent: evocative sensory memories of morning meals and the variety and flavor inherent in this class of baking. Growing up in Switzerland, I experienced a culture that revered its bakers and homemakers alike, where each day began with something hot from the oven. Whether it came from the corner bakery or was made by Mom, it was made with care from fresh, local ingredients. A typical Sunday morning featured the laughter and conversation of relatives and friends mingling around a table spread with croissants, rolls, and braided bread; complemented by a savory platter of cheeses, smoked meats, spreads, and jars of sweet butters, jams, and honey.

Despite this book's title, its scope is not limited to the morning meal. Breads and pastries traditionally enjoyed during these hours tend toward the sweeter side, which makes them perfect for afternoon tea as well. But sweetness is not a prerequisite; there are many savory versions of these recipes that highlight the flavors of cheeses, vegetables, and smoked meats,

to name a few. These are wonderful additions to a brunch menu and accompany soups, salads, and light dinners perfectly.

FINDING TIME FOR BAKING

We live in a busy time. It used to be that most people could find a moment of quiet each morning or pause for a midday break. Now, most of our days are scheduled to the max. From the moment the alarm clock jars us awake, we begin a choreographed daily routine executed with military precision. A harried series of showers, dressing, and lunch making precedes the drive to work or school with scarcely a minute to spare. Then the afternoon scramble of errands and chauffeuring children to their activities begins. (Some of us miraculously squeeze in a workout.) No wonder we often resort to drive-throughs and sandwich shops in between. A relaxing gathering at the kitchen table is nothing more than a distant memory of days gone by—or a wistful dream for the future. Homemade baked goods? They seem to be the pinnacle of indulgence.

I have some good news: You can have your life, however crazy it may be, and enjoy your own homemade baked goods, too!

With Baking Artisan Pastries and Breads *as your guide,*

You don't have to settle for the snack bar's offerings filled with artificial ingredients, or for the insipid, trans-fat-laden muffin. With *Baking Artisan Pastries and Breads* as your guide, you are on the way to enjoying your day just a little bit more. As with any hobby, you will need to spend some time practicing in the kitchen, and you should have an interest in baking and the desire to learn more. You are a part of a growing group of people who, be it from financial necessity or a desire to simplify their life and reconnect with family and friends, are getting back to the basics by spending more time at home and in the kitchen.

NAVIGATING THIS BOOK

Part One imparts basic information and lays the foundation for key baking components, such as ingredients, equipment, and techniques. You will learn what to look for when shopping for ingredients or choosing a mixer and other equipment. The basic techniques are explained in clear, step-by-step photographs and further illustrated in the enclosed DVD, which provides invaluable visual instruction on mixing, shaping, and other techniques.

Armed with this knowledge, you can progress with confidence into Part Two, which features more than thirty mouth-watering bread and pastry recipes. The recipes (and their techniques) progress from simple to more complex. You'll reach nearly immediate gratification when you sample quick breads, muffins, and scones, and you will build confidence as you explore the more challenging territory of yeasted, enriched, and laminated doughs. These products require a bit more work, but are flavorful and rewarding.

Baking Artisan Pastries and Breads caters to all breakfast needs: from muffins ready within the hour to more decadent treats, such as lemon brioche doughnuts and chocolate croissants. Whether your goal is to bake simple and wholesome treats to tuck away for lunch-box snacks or to craft a pastry menu that rivals that of any upscale hotel, it is my hope that you are encouraged and inspired by these pages.

Happy Baking!

you're on your way to savoring sweets even more.

PART ONE

Basics

UNDERSTANDING BASIC CONCEPTS and mastering certain fundamental techniques is the obvious first step to success in baking, yet it can be so tempting to jump ahead to the "fun stuff." Trust me: while baking is an art, it is also a science, and the time it takes to carefully review the basics in Part One will be well invested! As in any skilled discipline, it is important to build a solid foundation first—it will only add to your overall baking enjoyment and satisfaction.

The following chapters explain in detail the essential ingredients and equipment and teach the basic techniques that are utilized throughout the book. Because everyone's time is precious, the core concepts are presented in a simple, straightforward manner, arming you with the confidence to get you into the kitchen quickly to begin baking!

CHAPTER ONE

Ingredients

Compared with bread baking's long tradition of working with just four staples—flour, water, salt, and yeast—baking pastries and breads (and beyond) incorporates a far wider range of ingredients. Not only does it rely on the "fundamental four," but it also expands into the world of sweeteners, fats, chemical leavening agents, eggs, and flavorings. Clearly, this creates countless possibilities for flavors and variety—a most welcome treat for your morning taste buds!

Part of the fun of baking, in my opinion, is shopping for and selecting the ingredients. These days there seem to be countless choices: from broadly stocked supermarkets to small local farmers' markets and natural food stores, and even the vast Internet, your options are wide and varied. Much of this stems from the heightened awareness and public interest surrounding the source of what we eat; its origin, the manner in which it was grown or manufactured, and the distance it traveled are all factors many people consider when purchasing food, particularly fresh produce.

Most of the ingredients in the formulas are easy to find and many are likely to be on hand in your pantry, but a few might require a special shopping trip, depending on your local resources. Always buy the best-quality ingredients that you can comfortably afford—the results will be well worth it! And by all means, experiment with different brands and sources . . . you may find a new favorite quite unexpectedly.

The following pages will familiarize you with the major ingredients of baking and the important roles each plays within a formula. You'll learn the "how" and "why" behind some of the magic that occurs during the baking process and will come to appreciate the science behind the art. It is my hope that this newfound knowledge will empower you when it comes time to dive into the actual baking.

Flour

Flour is considered the backbone and structure of baked goods, so it is a natural ingredient with which to start. The basic definition of *flour* is simply a cereal grain ground into a powder form. Depending on the region or culinary tradition, that grain can vary. Corn flour is a staple of Latin American cuisine, while rice flour is the cornerstone of Asian noodles and baking. Other types of flour are often used in conjunction with wheat flour; for example, rye flour is a standard ingredient in the dark sourdough breads of Germany and Scandinavia. In North America and Europe, wheat flour is the main type of flour. As the baking in this book has its origins in the European tradition of bread baking, the attention will focus on varieties of wheat flour.

Wheat is grown in many different places throughout the world, and the resulting flour is as unique as the environment from which it originates, with the region, temperature, and humidity all playing a role. Professional bakers in the United States have embraced a milling classification system that profiles the characteristics of wheat flour. For example, it's not unusual for bakers to order a particular flour from their supplier based on the species of wheat and when it is grown, or the protein and ash contents. Flour companies create specific blends of flours, such as all-purpose, bread, and cake flours, which are suitable for many noncommercial uses at home.

Flour is created by milling the wheat seed, known as the wheat kernel or wheat berry, into fine particles. The kernel comprises three main parts: the bran, endosperm, and the germ. The *bran* is the protective hard outer layer of the seed and is very high in dietary fiber. Below this layer lies the endosperm, which makes up the bulk of the wheat kernel (over 80 percent). This is the whitest part of the kernel and includes the most starch. The *endosperm* also contains the two gluten-forming proteins, *glutenin* and *gliadin*, which are unique to wheat flour and are critical in forming the network of gluten, an important structure of baked goods. The *germ* is the embryo of the wheat plant, and under the right conditions will germinate—or sprout—into a new plant.

Wheat berries (left), whole wheat flour (middle), and bread flour (right)

It is very small but highly concentrated in protein, vitamins, and minerals.

During the milling process, the wheat kernel is crushed into progressively smaller particles and sifted, depending on the type of flour to be milled. Whole wheat flour contains all three parts of the kernel (hence the name *whole wheat*), whereas white flour (refined flour) is milled only from the endosperm. The degree of separation that takes place is referred to as the *extraction rate*. A flour using the entire wheat kernel is said to have a 100 percent extraction rate. As a general rule, the higher the extraction rate a flour has, the more minerals and nutrition it contains. Most conventional artisan bread flours and all-purpose flours have an extraction rate of about 73 to 76 percent.

After milling, the flour enters a maturing process that takes one of two routes: naturally or through the addition of bleaching or maturing agents. When a flour is aged naturally, air is incorporated into it. The oxygen in the air oxidizes the pigments in the flour, making them whiter. It also oxidizes the gluten-forming proteins, allowing them to build a stronger gluten network. Naturally aged flours are often referred to as *unbleached* and are the preferred choice of artisan bakers. Because the natural aging process requires that the flours take up precious time in silo space, some suppliers artificially age the flour by treating it with bleaching or maturing agents, such as benzoyl peroxide, chlorine, or potassium bromate. Flours that are chemically aged have been *bleached* and/or *bromated*. These agents have harmful side effects on both humans and the environment; when in doubt, choose unbleached and unbromated flour if possible.

If you talk shop with artisan bread bakers, it won't take long before they start rattling off about different attributes of flours, from the protein and ash content to the moisture content and wheat type. Although it's good to know that these speci-

A soft cake flour lumps up after squeezing (left), whereas a bread flour does not compact (right).

fications exist for the professionals, it is not necessary to get bogged down with or intimidated by such data. Luckily, when you go to the store to buy flour, you can usually find several different brands and types upon the shelves, handily packaged according to their intended use. Don't be overwhelmed by the selection; the recipes in this book were all formulated using a quality flour (with a protein content ideally around 11 to 12 percent) or whole wheat flour (ideal protein content of 14 percent). Bread flour is typically milled from a hard winter wheat and, when squeezed, does not lump up in the hand and therefore does not require sifting. In addition, all-purpose flour performs well in quick breads where gluten formation is not as important, but can also be used in yeasted doughs with some minor adjustments (see page 18).

The Whole Wheat FACTOR

If you are seeking some additional health and hardiness, you can easily substitute up to 25 percent of the weight of bread flour with whole wheat flour. Be sure to have a bit of extra liquid on hand during the initial mixing process—the wheat bran tends to absorb more water during the bulk fermentation stage.

Flour should be stored in an airtight container away from heat. To ensure freshness and quality, buy only as much flour to last you 2 or 3 months at a time. If need be, flour can be wrapped tightly in plastic wrap and stored in the freezer for up to 1 year. Because whole wheat flour contains the natural oils of the wheat germ, it is more sensitive to heat than is regular bread or all-purpose flour. Therefore, special consideration should be taken when storing whole wheat flour. It is best stored in an airtight container in the refrigerator, especially during warm spells, to prevent the flour from becoming rancid.

What's the Purpose of ALL-PURPOSE?

Professional bakers and pastry chefs keep many more types of flour on hand than home bakers do. They have the storage for these different types of flour—from bread to cake to whole wheat and more. For home bakers, all-purpose flour may not be the perfectly matched flour for every application, but it can be used in most home situations with some success.

You can substitute all-purpose flour for bread flour in any of these recipes; just keep in mind that the protein content is not quite as high and therefore the flour is not as strong. Protein molecules need water (or liquid) to hydrate, and so a bread flour with more protein will absorb more water than will an all-purpose flour (or any weaker flour). If you substitute all-purpose flour, reserve a bit of liquid during the initial mixing process to achieve a properly hydrated dough.

Sugars and Sweeteners

Despite its reputation, sugar does more than just sweeten things up. It tenderizes, helps retain moisture, improves shelf life, contributes to color and flavor, and provides food for yeast, among other functions. And you thought it was just to satisfy your sweet tooth.

Sugar is a carbohydrate. There are many different forms of sugar and they are classified according to their source. Fructose and glucose are found in fruits and vegetables, whereas lactose is in milk products. The white granulated sugar most commonly used in baking is *sucrose* and is derived primarily from two sources: sugarcane and sugar beets.

Sugarcane is a tall, reedy grass that began to be cultivated in the South Pacific over eight thousand years ago. Sugar beets grow in a more temperate climate than sugarcane and once the discovery was made that they could be used for sugar manufacturing, sugar beets became the crop of choice for the European and American source of sugar. White granulated sugar, the type most used in baking, goes through a two-step manufacturing process. The sugar is first extracted or milled from its source (either sugarcane or sugar beets) into a crude, raw sugar. It then travels to a refinery plant, where this raw sugar is refined in stages into pure white sugar.

Sweeteners can be divided into two groups: dry crystalline sugar and syrups. All sugars (both crystalline and syrups) are *hygroscopic* to some degree, meaning that they attract and retain moisture. This is a key concept to understanding the behavior of sugars within a recipe.

Once dissolved, sugar acts as a tenderizer; it delays the formation of structure by interfering with some of the other processes. Because gluten, egg, and starch structure all require water, the hygroscopic quality of sugar slows down their formation by drawing water away from these builders. So, the more sugar present in a recipe, the more tender the product will be. However, there needs to be a balance. If too much sugar is added, then little structure will form at all, resulting in little or no rise in the product or the product's collapsing as it cools.

Because sugar attracts water, it increases the softness and moistness of a product, a desirable characteristic in many cakes, cookies, and quick breads. This moisture retention helps to extend the shelf life by preventing drying and staling from occurring too quickly.

When heated to high temperatures during the baking process, sugars go through a caramelization process that simultaneously contributes a nice brown color as well as a warm caramelized flavor. Sometimes the sweetener possesses its own color before baking, such as with brown sugar, molasses, and honey, but these, too, will caramelize just the same.

As the formulas in chapters 5 and 6 (Enriched Dough and Laminated Dough) contain yeast, it is important to recognize the role sugar plays in the fermentation process. The fermentation process is complex and will be covered in more detail in chapter 3 in the Yeasted Dough Techniques section, but for now it is good to know that yeast feeds off and breaks down sugar, resulting in the formation of primarily carbon dioxide and alcohol. The sugar in the dough comes from both the starch carbohydrate from the flour as well as any other sugar added to the dough. The doughs for breakfast breads and pastries contain added sugar to help create the tender, flavorful products so welcome in the morning hours.

Clockwise from left: powdered sugar, granulated sugar, light brown sugar, raw sugar, corn syrup, and honey

Granulated Sugar

This is the type of refined sugar that most people consider the standard for sugar. It is white because all of the molasses and impurities have been removed during the refining process. It is available in several different textures, including a finely ground grade, known in Great Britain as *castor* sugar and in the United States as *superfine* sugar, which dissolves quickly and incorporates smoothly into batters and creams. Some granulated sugars are semirefined, meaning they have not gone through as many refining cycles as pure white sugar and have not been filtered to decolorize; known as *turbinado* sugars, they have a pale golden color and a mild flavor and will function in baked goods as regular sugar does.

Brown Sugar

True brown sugar in its original form is a partially refined sugar that retains some of the molasses to give it its color and somewhat moist texture. Typically it is commercially manufactured by mixing some molasses back into the refined sugar. It comes in light and dark brown varieties and needs to be stored in an airtight container for it to retain its softness and moisture.

The BROWN SUGAR BLUES

Some people store a piece of bread or apple slice in their brown sugar to help keep it moist, but if your brown sugar has dried out and become hard—don't despair! Put the bowl of brown sugar next to a small bowl of water in the microwave and heat for one minute. Check the texture and repeat if necessary. Alternatively, put the sugar into a baking dish and into a 250°F (120°C) oven. Let it heat for 5 minutes or until soft.

Powdered Sugar

Also known as *confectioners'* sugar, this sugar consists of sucrose crystals pulverized into a powder even finer than castor sugar. It is available in different levels of fineness usually indicated by 6X or 10X (the higher the number, the finer the powder). A 10X is good for icings and confections, whereas a 6X is suitable for decorative dusting. Powdered sugar typically contains about 3 percent cornstarch to prevent caking.

Corn Syrup

Light corn syrup is made from cornstarch through the addition of enzymes. It is a natural product frequently used in the baking industry for its economical sweetening value and it helps to retain moisture in baked goods. Dark corn syrup is also available; it contains added molasses, coloring, and flavoring.

Honey

This natural sweetener is made from flower nectar by honey bees and was probably the first sweetener used by man. Even though the production of honey is accomplished by bees, the harvesting of honey is a time-consuming job done by people and involves many different steps. As a result, it is a relatively expensive ingredient and is used primarily for its unique flavor. The most common honeys are clover honey and orange blossom honey.

Other Syrups

Many other syrups are used in baking, including maple syrup, malt syrup, and molasses. Each brings a unique flavor profile to the mix of ingredients. You can experiment with substitutions, keeping in mind that the sweetness factor will not necessarily be the same (for example, maple syrup is sweeter than honey).

Fats

We live in a world where just the mention of the word *fat* will send shivers down the spine of the diet-conscious. Although they may sound unappetizing, fats and oils are a critical part of a balanced baking formula. It is important to understand how they work and to use them properly while considering the health concerns that are often associated with them.

The complex world of fats involves a good amount of science, some of which can seem very technical. Fats perform several different functions in baking. One of their main functions is to act as a tenderizer. Whereas sugar tenderizes by attracting water and drawing it away from the flour protein, fat prevents the water from coming into contact with the flour in the first place. When fat is introduced, it coats the flour protein with a pro-tective layer and partially "waterproofs" it. This shortens the gluten strands and the resulting crumb structure is tender and easy to chew.

Fat also plays an important role in the leavening process. When butter (or margarine or shortening) is creamed, the creaming process incorporates tiny air bubbles into the fat. These encapsulated air cells contribute to the lift that occurs during the baking process of cookies and cakes. Some fats, such as butter and margarine, have a small percentage of water as well, and certain recipes and techniques capitalize on this quality to help in leavening. Puff pastry and laminated doughs comprise a multitude of layers alternating fat and dough. The fat keeps the dough layers separated and, when the pastry is baked, the water in both the dough and butter turns to steam and further expands the layers, creating a nice flaky texture.

Clockwise from left: olive oil, vegetable oil, shortening, and butter

Additional functions of fats include contributing to both the moistness and flavor of a product as well as extending shelf life. In general, fats that are more liquid, such as oils, have more of a significant effect on the moistness of a product. All fats add a certain richness to a product, but a major reason for baking with butter is its unsurpassed flavor. Fats also slow down the staling process through increased moistness and by hindering the drying that results in a hard, crumbly texture of a stale product.

Butter

Butter is a dairy product made when butterfat solids are separated from heavy cream. Although it functions as most fats do by tenderizing and increasing moistness, its popularity among bakers is due to its rich flavor and smooth, melt-in-your-mouth texture. Butter has several disadvantages: it is expensive compared to other fats, it is the most difficult to work with due to its low melting point, it spoils faster than other fats, and it contains both saturated fat and cholesterol. Despite all this, butter imparts a richer crust and crumb color with a fuller flavor and aroma than other fats, making it the fat of choice of many bakers. Most of the time, I recommend butter when a solid fat is called for in a recipe.

Most butter sold in the United States contains about 80 percent fat, 15 percent water, and 5 percent milk solids. European-style butter has a minimum of 82 percent fat and is becoming more widely available to the home baker in the United States through specialty stores. Butters are classified as either *sweet cream* butter or *cultured* butter (made from sour cream). Sweet cream butters have no sweeteners added; they are not made from cream that has been soured. Butter can be salted or unsalted, with bakers and pastry chefs preferring the unsalted variety for several reasons, one of them being the fact that the salt content can vary from brand to brand, making it difficult to consis-tently adjust for taste in the formula. Even though it is more perishable than salted butter, unsalted butter has a fresher, sweeter flavor.

Even if you are not "rolling in dough," I recommend spending the extra time and money to procure an unsalted European butter with 82 percent butterfat whenever you make a laminated dough (see chapter 6). The water content in standard butter can be problematic during the rolling process; it tends to separate from the fat, resulting in fractures—an extremely frustrating addition to the already challenging lamination process.

Margarine

Margarine is made from either hydrogenated vegetable or animal fat and is a butter substitute. It has always been considered an inferior product, although some bakers and pastry chefs blend it with butter to reduce costs. By law, margarines must contain at least 80 percent fat. Those products that contain less than 80 percent are frequently referred to as low-fat, fat-free, or reduced-fat margarines or "spreads" and are not suitable butter substitutes.

Shortening

Shortenings are usually manufactured from hydrogenated vegetable oil, although animal fat can also be used either alone or in combination as well. Unlike butter or margarine, shortening has a fat content of 100 percent. Originally developed as a substitute for lard, shortening is white and tasteless, with a waxy mouth-feel. Its name is derived from its baking function: the fat covers the flour protein and "shortens" the development of the gluten strands. It has a high melting point and a good creaming ability, and is therefore used a lot in bakeries to make products mixed by creaming, such as cookies and quick breads. It is much less expensive than butter and is sometimes blended with butter to reduce the cost of products.

Oils

Oils are fats that are liquid at room temperature; oils used in baking are extracted from a vegetable source and are 100 percent fat. The most common source of vegetable oil is soybean, but it is also made from cottonseed, corn, canola, or peanuts. It does not contribute to leavening in the way that solid fats do, for two reasons: one, it contains no air or water to escape and create lift or volume during the baking process, and two, because of its liquid nature, it does not hold or trap air bubbles (as solid fats do when they are creamed). This makes them suitable only for recipes using the blending method, such as quick breads, and sometimes for the rubbing method used with certain types of pie dough.

Olive oil is used judiciously in baking. It has a distinct flavor most commonly used in making focaccia, pizza, savory flatbreads, and some other yeasted doughs. It is not very common in sweeter breads, although it appears in some regional sweets such as Mediterranean desserts or the French gibassier formula (see page 115). Because it is high in monounsaturated fats, olive oil has become one of the oils of choice for a healthy lifestyle. A virgin olive oil is squeezed and separated from the olives without using any heat and without altering the natural oil in any way. Extra-virgin olive oil is the highest-quality olive oil available. However, the superior flavor in extra-virgin olive oil is extremely susceptible to high heat. Therefore with high-heat applications, a virgin olive oil or even a refined olive oil may be a better choice.

Transitioning away from TRANS FATS

Fat comes in four forms: monounsaturated fat, polyunsaturated fat, saturated fat, and trans fat. Our bodies need mono- and polyunsaturated fats to function properly, and our consumption of saturated fats should be kept low. But, when it comes to trans fats, there is nothing good to report.

Trans fats have rocketed to the forefront of health concerns, and rightly so. These fats are the worst kind, and while they increase the shelf life of some products, they do nothing but decrease our own. Partially hydrogenated vegetable oils are the worst villains —not the small amounts of naturally occurring trans fats found in meat and dairy products and in some fruits and vegetables.

Shortenings, margarines, and commercial lards traditionally fall into this category, although some now contain less than 0.5 grams of trans fat per serving and can be technically classified as "trans fat free" under the Food and Drug Administration guidelines. I still recommend using butter. You should be able to successfully substitute it in equal amounts for the shortening or margarine in your favorite family recipes.

Leaveners

A *leavener* is a substance that introduces volume into a product; in baking, the three main leaveners are gases: steam (water vapor), air, and carbon dioxide (CO_2). Ingredients that are introduced as catalysts for the leavening process are also called leaveners or *leavening agents*. Leavening agents can be divided into two categories: natural (or biological) leaveners and chemical leaveners. Before going any further, let's take a general look at what happens in the oven during baking.

Clockwise from top right: fresh yeast, baking powder, instant yeast, baking soda

First, conjure up a bit of high school chemistry. Matter comes in three forms: solids, liquids, and gases. A change in temperature can change matter from one form to another. For example, ice (solid) melts into water (liquid), which evaporates into steam (gas). As the temperature increases, molecules move progressively faster and expand away from each other; it is this expansion process that is the basis for leavening. During the baking process, the heat from the oven cause the gases to expand outward, pushing on the cells of the dough or batter and increasing the volume.

The three gaseous leaveners are introduced or encouraged in the formulas in different manners. Steam is the gaseous form of water, so an ingredient that contains any amount of moisture (water, milk, eggs, syrups, and so on) will give off a certain amount of steam when heated. Air is incorporated into doughs and batters through mixing techniques, including creaming and whipping. Carbon dioxide, the only one of the three gases that is not present in all batters and doughs, is formed by the chemical reaction that takes place either during fermentation or through the addition of chemical leavening agents. Because carbon dioxide plays such an important role in leavening, the leavening agents involved with the creation of carbon dioxide deserve some special attention.

Natural Leavening Agents

Yeast is a natural, or biological, leavening agent that produces carbon dioxide during the fermentation process. Yeast cells are alive; they are tiny microorganisms that feed on sugars to survive. Wild yeast cells, *Candida milleri*, are present all around us and can be "captured" and grown for baking, as they are in a sourdough culture. More commonly, another strain of yeast, *Saccharomyces cerevsiae*, is commercially manufactured under strict laboratory growing conditions then sold in the form of instant yeast, fresh compressed yeast, or active dry yeast. Both forms of yeast, whether wild or commercially manufactured, are considered natural leavening agents. As the yeast consumes the sugar during the fermentation process, carbon dioxide is produced as a by-product; this is what creates the gas bubbles within the dough or batter (see more on this process in the Yeasted Dough Techniques section of chapter 3).

Yeast is commercially available in the following three forms:

FRESH YEAST: Fresh, or compressed, yeast contains 70 percent water and is sold in brick form. Quality fresh yeast is tan in color; has a pleasant, yeasty odor; and breaks off cleanly when touched. It can be purchased in some grocery stores and through catalog and Internet sources. Because it is fresh, it needs to be stored in an airtight container in the refrigerator, where it has a shelf life of about 3 weeks. For a bakery that produces a lot of product and goes through yeast fairly quickly, fresh yeast can be a good match. But for the home baker who only bakes occasionally and in smaller quantities, fresh yeast often goes bad before it is used up. Plus, one can never be quite certain how long the yeast was on the store shelf before it was purchased in the first place, making the shelf life at home even less predictable.

Special Yeast for SWEET BAKING

Yeasted sweet breakfast breads and pastries are abundant in rich ingredients such as sugar, milk, eggs, and fat, and do not contain as much readily available moisture as standard doughs. As a result, the flour, sugar, and yeast compete with one another for the liquids. The amount of regular yeast is increased to give it a fighting chance against the others.

This is where the "high octane" version of yeast steps in: Osmotolerant yeast is specially selected to work within this harsh competitive environment so that proper fermentation can occur within the desired time. It usually needs to be special ordered through a catalog or website (see Resources, page 168). Be assured, though, that if all you have on hand is standard instant yeast, your dough will still ferment—it just might be a bit slower.

DRY ACTIVE YEAST: This type of yeast is probably the most familiar to home bakers and is readily available in supermarkets. Developed in the 1940s, it simplified bread baking at home but was never adopted by professional bakers due to its inferior performance compared with that of fresh yeast. It is sold in perforated envelopes and needs to be properly rehydrated before use. The yeast is first dissolved for about 5 minutes in a warm (100°F/38°C) liquid (water in most cases) before adding to the final dough. If the formula calls for water to be added at a cooler temperature when added to the final dough, then the liquid yeast slurry should be allowed to cool as well before mixing can commence.

INSTANT YEAST: Developed in the late 1970s, instant yeast combines the convenience of dry yeast with the performance of fresh. It is sold in packaged envelopes or vacuum-packed bricks and is referred to by some manufacturers as "bread machine yeast" or "rapid rise yeast." It has a long shelf life and can be stored unopened without refrigeration for up to a year, but once opened it should be stored in an airtight container in the refrigerator. Manufacturers recommend using the instant yeast within one month, but my own personal experience indicates it can be stored for *much* longer. Instant yeast does not need to be dissolved and can be incorporated along with the dry ingredients of a final dough before mixing. Instant yeast is increasingly becoming the yeast of choice for many baking professionals and serious home bakers alike, due to its reliable performance.

Instant yeast is also available in an *osmotolerant* form for use in many of the sweeter enriched doughs found in this book. These doughs contain a higher percentage of sugar than regular lean bread doughs, and the hygroscopic quality of the sugar draws the moisture away from the yeast, making it more difficult for the yeast to grow. The osmotolerant yeast has been formulated to perform under these harsh conditions and is therefore ideal to use for some recipes.

Chemical Leavening Agents

Alternatively, carbon dioxide can also be created through the addition of chemical leaveners. These include baking soda and baking powder (and baking ammonia, more commonly found in Europe). These leaveners break down in the presence of moisture and/or heat and produce carbon dioxide gas in the process.

BAKING SODA

Baking soda, otherwise known as sodium bicarbonate, is a common chemical leavener. Baking soda alone cannot do the trick; for baking soda to create carbon dioxide, it needs to combine with both moisture and some type of acid. The acid comes in the form of another ingredient, such as buttermilk, yogurt, sour cream, unsweetened chocolate, natural cocoa, vinegar, fruits and their juices, brown sugar, honey, or maple syrup. The acid reacts with the baking soda in the presence of moisture and enables the baking soda to break down more quickly into carbon dioxide, water, and salt residue. If too much baking soda is used, the excess salt residue can be detected as an off flavor in the product. When leavening with baking soda, it is important to bake immediately upon mixing since the acidic ingredients react practically instantaneously.

BAKING POWDER

Baking powder is essentially baking soda pre-mixed with an acid (usually cream of tartar). When combined with water, baking powder breaks down to release carbon dioxide. These days, all baking powders available to the home baker are known as *double-acting*, meaning that one part of the baking powder (about two-thirds) starts to react with the moisture in the formula and the remaining part (about one-third) reacts with the heat of the oven. This extends the window of time during which the product can be leavened.

TESTING Your Baking Powder and Baking Soda

To check if your baking powder or baking soda still has the power to make your baked goods rise, here are two simple tests: For baking powder, stir ½ teaspoon (2.5 g) into 2 tablespoons (28 ml) of hot water. For baking soda, stir ½ teaspoon (2.5 g) into 2 tablespoons (28 ml) of vinegar or lemon juice. If they are still working, they will bubble and fizz; if not, then it's time to buy a new box.

Homemade Baking Powder

If you open your cupboard and realize you are out of baking powder (or what you have has lost its power), don't despair—you can make your own. To make the equivalent of 1 teaspoon (5 g) of baking powder, mix ½ teaspoon (2.5 g) of baking soda together with ¼ teaspoon (1.2 g) of cream of tartar. Both of these ingredients keep indefinitely when stored separately, so it is a good idea to have them on hand for such emergencies.

Eggs

No other ingredient quite compares to an egg; it is one of nature's nutritional miracles and its unique qualities make it indispensable in the bakeshop. Besides its nutritional value, the egg adds flavor, richness, and color, and serves many other functions in baked goods. When whipped or beaten, eggs are a leavening agent by trapping air cells which expand when heated. When eggs are creamed along with butter, they help to encapsulate even more air than otherwise possible. Eggs act as a tenderizer, as the fat in the yolk contributes to the shortening of gluten strands. Lecithin, an emulsifier, found in the yolk, allows fillings and sauces to bind together and thicken. And the moisture in eggs allows them to act as a binding agent and help retain moisture in the product, thereby extending the shelf life.

SEPARATING Eggs

It's best to separate eggs when they are cold since the yolk doesn't break as easily then. Crack the egg in the middle and work over a small bowl to gently pry the egg open. Keep the yolk in one half of the eggshell while the whites drip into the bowl. Carefully transfer the yolk back and forth between shells to release as much of the whites as possible into the bowl, then place the separated yolk in another bowl. Another technique is to cup the egg in your hand and let the whites run down into a bowl through your fingers. You definitely need a cold egg and clean hand for this technique!

Eggshells come in a natural rainbow of colors which differ depending on the variety of hen.

The egg's hard outer shell protects its fragile innards and is made from calcium carbonate. The shell's color varies by the breed of the chicken, from a chocolate brown to a creamy white to even shades of blue and green. The color of the shell has no relationship to the quality or taste of the egg. Eggshells are porous and over time eggs lose their moisture and absorb air (along with flavors and odors). The white of the egg contains water and protein along with some trace minerals. Raw egg whites are clear and coagulate to opaque white when heated. When whipped, the protein and the water in egg whites bond together to form a stable foam. Egg yolks can be pale yellow to bright orange, depending on the diet of the hen. Along with protein, vitamins, and minerals, the yolks contain all the fat, cholesterol, and most of the calories.

Fresh eggs come in a range of sizes, and unless noted, most recipes assume the use of large eggs. Eggs should be stored in temperatures of less than 41°F (5°C) and have a shelf life of approximately 4 weeks.

How to FREEZE EGGS

Eggs can be frozen, but not in their shell. To freeze whole eggs, crack them into a bowl and stir gently (do not try to incorporate any air.) Pour into a plastic freezer bag and label with the date then freeze. If you end up with extra whites or yolks from a recipe, you can freeze those as well. Egg whites can simply be frozen as they are, either in plastic freezer bags or first in ice-cube trays and then in freezer bags. Egg yolks need to have a small amount of either salt (½ teaspoon [3 g] per 1 cup [235 ml] of egg) or sugar (1 tablespoon [14 g] per 1 cup [235 ml] of egg) blended in to inhibit them from getting lumpy during storage. Frozen eggs in all forms last up to a year in the freezer and should be thawed in the refrigerator the day before using. Only use thawed eggs in dishes or baked goods that are thoroughly cooked or baked.

Flavorings

Ingredients contribute their own unique flavors to a formula, and sometimes they dictate the flavor. After all, what's a banana bread without the bananas? The experience of flavor has three parts: taste, chemical feeling, and aroma. Basic taste sensations are perceived in the mouth and include sweet, salty, sour, and bitter. The chemical feeling factors include the burn of cinnamon, the cooling of mint, and the sting of alcohol. The smell, or aroma, is the most complex (chemically speaking) and considered to be the most important of the components of flavor.

In this section, the flavorings covered are those that enhance the flavors of the main ingredients and round out the tasting experience, such as extracts, liquors, spices, and herbs.

Salt

Salt modifies and enhances flavor in all foods, including baked goods. It serves other essential functions as well, particularly in bread dough. It comes in a variety of forms (table salt, iodized salt, kosher salt, sea salt, and so on) from a variety of sources (salt mines or from the sea).

Salt is one of the fundamental four ingredients in bread (flour, water, and yeast being the other three) and helps control the rate of yeast fermentation and enzymatic activity by slowing it down. It also helps to strengthen gluten, making the dough less sticky and more cohesive. As a result, the dough is easier to handle and the final product has better volume and a finer crumb.

Extracts

Extracts add concentrated, powerful flavor to food without adding excess liquid or changing the consistency. They are common in the home or bakery and are either natural or artificial, depending on the source of the flavor ingredient. Extracts contain alcohol, which "extracts" and dissolves the flavor ingredients and prevents microbial growth. Common extract flavors include vanilla, peppermint, orange, anise, lemon, almond, and ginger.

Vanilla is by far the most commonly used extract in baking. To make it, mashed vanilla beans (the seed pods of a particular orchid) are percolated with or macerated in diluted alcohol over a period of two or three weeks, extracting the vanilla flavor and absorbing it into the alcohol. The extract is filtered and aged. Vanilla connoisseurs often select vanilla extract based upon the variety of vanilla bean used in the extract or its origin, such as Bourbon, Tahitian, or Mexican. The Bourbon variety is the most commonly used variety in extracts.

Flavorings come in a variety of forms which enhance the tasting experience.

Compounds

These types of flavorings are more commonly used by the professional baker and pastry chef than the home baker. They are concentrated ingredients to which sugar and flavors are added. Compounds include fruit varieties (such as raspberry, strawberry, and lemon), nuts (such as almond marzipan), and vanilla paste. Quality and intensity vary from brand to brand and some compounds require refrigeration.

Spices

Spices, products made from dried plants usually grown in the tropics, are used mainly for seasoning. They can come from all different plant parts, including the seeds, berries, flowers, fruit, leaves, bark, and roots, and can be either whole or ground. Spices contain highly concentrated essential oils, which add robust flavors. Whole spices retain their flavor longer than ground spices. Spices should be stored in an airtight container and away from heat and light. The quality of spices can vary greatly depending on the growing conditions, harvesting method, plant variety, manufacturing processes, and the age and storage conditions of the spice. If a spice has lost its aroma and pungency, throw it out and replace it.

Liqueurs

Liqueurs are similar to extracts; they are alcohol based but contain more sugar and other ingredients. Regular liqueurs are designed to be palatable for drinking and are therefore not as concentrated as extracts. Some liqueurs used in the baking industry are designed to be more concentrated than normal. Liqueurs come in different flavors, including coffee, hazelnut, almond, chocolate, cherry, and pear. The flavor and intensity varies from brand to brand, and price is not always an indication of quality; sometimes the one you prefer to drink is not the one you would wish to use in baking.

Herbs

Fresh herbs have full, clean flavor, but dried herbs are more concentrated than fresh herbs, readily available year round, and have a long shelf life. They are easily incorporated into savory baked goods and desserts. Dried herbs should be stored like spices: in an airtight container and away from light and heat. Fresh herbs should be rinsed and patted dry before loosely wrapping them in a damp paper towel and storing in the refrigerator to prolong freshness.

CHAPTER TWO

Equipment

WITH EQUIPMENT, QUALITY COUNTS. Any professional baker or pastry chef will tell you that a kitchen stocked with basic durable bakeware will provide years of baking joy and satisfaction. It's easy to be seduced by fancy spreads in magazines that show designer kitchens with pristine pots and pans. If you have ever visited the bakeshop of a culinary school or had the opportunity to peek at a restaurant kitchen, then you know as well as I do that equipment gets used—and it doesn't necessarily look all that pretty. The truth is your baking equipment has a job to do, and the important thing is that it serves you well.

On the other hand, buying new equipment is necessary. You may be setting up your first kitchen, or you are buying a special piece for a new recipe, or maybe that chic "designer" pan didn't live up to its appearance. You may find yourself roaming the aisles at the kitchen specialty shop or leafing through that gourmet catalog wondering where to start and what to look for. It can be downright overwhelming.

This chapter covers the major pieces of equipment that the home baker may want to acquire. From the larger-ticket items of mixers and food processors to the smaller (yet most critical) tools of pastry brushes and spatulas and everything in between, you'll gain an understanding of the different options and styles available to you and the factors that might play into your decision-making process. Knowledge is power, and when you become informed, it's much easier to weed out the good from the mediocre and purchase with confidence.

As a general note, I believe in making use of what you have on hand for equipment and tools, replacing them only when it is absolutely necessary. If they are still usable, pass along items that you are replacing to those in need—many non-profit organizations or shelters would happily accept your older equipment.

Scales

In my opinion, a good-quality scale is the most important piece of equipment a baker can own. Baking is grounded in science and products are formed through the precise combination of ingredients, which results in certain harmonious chemical reactions. In this respect, a bakeshop is akin to a science lab where every experiment is a balance of specific ratios of ingredients . . . and precision counts! Portions of ingredients can be measured much more accurately with a quality scale than with measuring cups, ensuring a more consistent product.

Ideally, a scale used for bread baking should have a 5 kilogram capacity (5,000 grams) and measure in 1 gram increments. Generally, the larger the capacity and the smaller the increment of measure, the more expensive the scale. Different types of scales are available to the home baker: digital, compression, and balance. I prefer to use a digital scale. They are compact and take up little space when stored, are very accurate and easy to use, and have some nice digital functions. For easy cleaning, look for a large, removable scaling surface made from stainless steel. A large display area will make reading the numbers easy and a tare, or zero, function will make the successive measurement of ingredients seamless. *Compression scales* work via spring mechanism and are not uniformly accurate, especially those that are cheaply made. Measuring smaller amounts of ingredients is especially difficult. A good set of measuring cups and spoons can be more accurate. *Balance scales* compare the ingredients to be weighed against incremental weights. These are the types of scales associated with chemistry classes or physician's offices. They are accurate but cumbersome to work with in the kitchen.

Mixers

The second most important piece of baking equipment is a mixer. There are two basic types for bread baking: a stand mixer and a spiral mixer. Each has a distinctly different way of moving and kneading the dough. A stand mixer has a rotating attachment that combines the ingredients in a stationary bowl. A spiral mixer not only has a rotating attachment, but the bowl rotates as well.

A compression scale (left) and a digital scale (right)

Stand Mixer

These are the most common mixers available to home bakers. They come in many colors and sizes and are capable of a variety of tasks. From whipping egg whites and cream to mixing a cake batter to kneading a bread dough, a stand mixer is considered a staple piece of equipment in the kitchen. However, the mixing action of this workhorse can be a little aggressive with bread dough. Many professional bread bakers choose to mix their doughs in a spiral mixer.

Spiral Mixer

A spiral mixer delicately develops gluten structure within a dough. It mimics the hand mixing process more accurately than a stand mixer does, and does it more efficiently. However, it has one major drawback: the attachment is permanent and cannot be removed, thereby limiting its application strictly to mixing dough. Spiral mixers are usually preferred for mixing yeasted dough. Some smaller versions are becoming available, but at quite a hefty price tag. If you are very serious about bread baking and do a lot of it, you may want to consider splurging on a spiral mixer someday, but a well-designed stand mixer does the job sufficiently and at a much more affordable price.

The recipes in this book are optimally formulated with a stand mixer in mind. When buying a mixer, look for one that has a minimum 5-quart (5 L) bowl capacity. Do not be misled in thinking that a higher-wattage machine is going to give you more mixing power; this is not necessarily true. The advertised wattage is a measurement of the input wattage, or the electricity flowing into the machine. It is best to do your research, shop around, and seek out opinions to make an informed purchasing decision.

If you know you are going to use your mixer to make bread dough, pay careful attention to the design of the dough hook as well as to the tolerance between the bottom of the dough hook and the bowl. A good dough hook has some fairly complex bends and angles designed to move the dough in a kneading motion. A graceful curve may look nice but is not nearly as effective. A dough hook that comes close to the bottom of the bowl will have the ability to incorporate all the ingredients more efficiently and will reduce the amount of time spent scraping the hook and the bowl.

A 5-quart (5 L) stand mixer is a popular choice for home bakers.

Mixer Attachments

There are three classic mixer attachments:

WHIP

A whisk attachment is used for whipping eggs, cream, and other aerated mixtures for cakes, mousses, and cream desserts. It is too delicate for batters and doughs.

PADDLE

This all-purpose attachment is ideal for creaming, blending, or rubbing ingredients. The closer the paddle comes to the bowl, the better incorporated the ingredients.

DOUGH HOOK

Designed specifically for dough mixing applications. Pay attention to shape of the hook and the space between the hook and the bowl. My dough hook designed with complex bends and angles can mix an enriched dough to complete development within 10 minutes and the other more graceful and curvilinear dough hook takes closer to 20 minutes to mix the same dough.

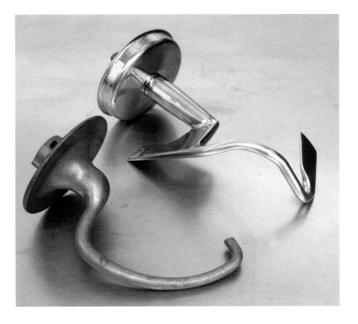

Ovens

Put simply, you can't bake without an oven. The good news: your kitchen most likely has one. There are four main types of ovens: conventional, convection, combination, and wood-fired. A *conventional oven* is heated by either gas or electric elements and has been the standard residential oven for years. A *convection oven* circulates the oven heat with a fan and distributes heat more evenly, resulting in a quicker cooking or baking time. A *combination oven* combines the features of both a conventional and convection oven; many newer oven models fit into this category. A *wood-fired oven* is a masonry oven built to capture and retain the heat and energy of a wood fire. Wood-fired ovens are great for artisan-style hearth breads, and smaller residential models designed for the artisan bread enthusiast are growing in popularity, but they take a completely different approach to baking bread not covered in this book.

For the formulas in this book, a convection oven or the convection mode in a combination oven is ideal. **If you are using a conventional oven, increase the baking temperature 20° to 40°F (10° to 20°C) more than the stated convection temperature.** It is also a good idea to check the calibration of your oven, since some ovens can be off as much as 50°F (10°C). An oven thermometer can indicate any discrepancies and then make the necessary adjustments. After some time, you will get to know your oven and its idiosyncrasies—where the hot spots are, for example, or how long it takes to preheat.

Dough hooks can vary greatly from mixer to mixer. The complex curves of the top hook make it more effective for mixing dough than the one below it.

Food Processors

A food processor is a versatile addition to any kitchen. It is indispensable for making nut flours and can grate and shred fruits, vegetables, cheese, and chocolate in seconds. Many have a blade designed for mixing yeasted bread doughs. Food processors come in different capacities (ranging from 2 to 20 cups [0.45 to 4.54 kg]) and the first step is to buy one that matches your needs: small batches of ingredients or preparing food for a small army? Power should be considered, too. Kneading dough is strenuous and will require a larger and more powerful model.

Baking Forms

Most breakfast breads are baked in a baking form: muffin tins to loaf pans to other specialty forms. Each shape, size, and material has its own advantages. If you find that you do not have the correct size indicated for the formula, you can usually make use of what you have on hand already, with some minor adjustments.

Metal

Metal baking forms include aluminum, stainless steel, and tin-plated steel. Aluminum forms are good conductors of heat and are best when made from a heavy gauge. All containers that have been tin-plated have to be treated carefully because they are prone to rust. You will need to prepare the forms before baking by spraying with a nonstick cooking spray or using another method. I always line metal loaf pans with parchment paper to ensure an easy release after baking—a time consuming process if you are baking in bulk. When cleaning the forms, it is acceptable to wipe them out with a damp rag, provided the product released cleanly. However, if you do wash with water and detergent, place them in the warmth of a recently heated oven to dry completely before storing, especially for those that are prone to rust. Some metal forms are coated with a nonstick material, such as Teflon, designed for easier cleanup. Although these products provide time-saving benefits, questions have been raised about the safety of nonstick cookware. Certain gases and chemicals are released from these coatings when heated beyond 500°F (250°C), and some consumer groups have petitioned for warning labels on nonstick cookware. As with any new technology, it is best to research and make an informed decision with which you feel comfortable.

A baker's collection of metal baking forms: tartlet forms, popover baking molds, loaf pans, and brioche tins

Ceramic baking forms

Silicone baking molds are nonstick and flexible.

A variety of paper molds is available to the baker.

Glass and Ceramic

Glass and ceramic forms are easier to keep clean than their metal counterparts, but do not conduct heat as quickly. Depending on the recipe, this may be desirable. However, with most baking applications, you will notice a difference in browning and baking time compared with metal forms.

Silicone

Silicone is a nonstick material used for baking forms. These lightweight, flexible forms are easy to clean and store, and you can literally push the products out of the forms. They tend to be more expensive, but they never need nonstick cooking spray or paper lining. Products baked in silicone molds do not seem to brown as well as they do in traditional metal forms. As with any nonstick technology, inform yourself about the benefits and potential risks before using.

Paper

Paper baking liners have come a long way from the simple cupcake liners. Some companies specialize in creating unique baking molds from decorative paper and cardboard. Previously only available to the trade, they can now be purchased by home bakers through specialty stores. Products are baked and packaged in one step, making it very appealing to use for holiday baking and gift giving. The papers have been treated with a nonstick solution, which may be of concern to some people.

Other Tools and Equipment

Sheet Pans

Sheet pans, or rimmed baking sheets, are durable pans with an ideal thickness and stability for even baking and safe handling. Invest in good sheet pans and with the proper care they will last you a lifetime of baking. I like the commercial half sheet pans (18 x 13 x 1 inch [46 x 33 x 2.5 cm]) available through restaurant supply stores.

Heavy-duty aluminum half sheet pans are indispensable when baking.

Measuring Cups

There are two basic types of measuring cups: those for measuring dry ingredients and those for measuring liquids. Wet and dry ingredients have different volume measurements, and therefore require different measuring cups for accuracy. Cups for measuring dry ingredients are often sold in sets of ¼, ⅓, ½, and 1 cup. A good-quality set of measuring cups should be well balanced and ideally nest inside each other for storage. Liquid ingredients are measured in clear graduated measuring cups often available in 1-, 2-, or 4-cup (235, 475, and 1140 ml) capacities. Both glass or plastic styles can be used in the microwave, and have a handle and a convenient spout to pour from.

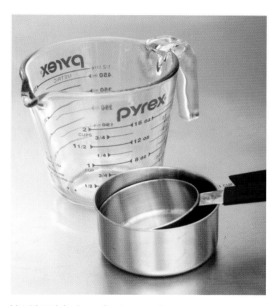

Liquid and dry ingredient measuring cups

Quality measuring spoons are durable, easy to use, and simply shaped.

Measuring Spoons

Sets of measuring spoons typically include ¼ teaspoon, ½ teaspoon, 1 teaspoon, and 1 tablespoon (1.25, 2.5, 5, and 15 ml) and are used to measure both wet and dry ingredients. I recommend a simple shape that will be easy to remove ingredients from and to clean.

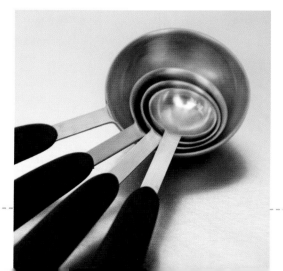

A timer is an essential tool for any kitchen.

Timers

A timer is an essential tool in the kitchen, no matter how good your memory. I often have several timers going at once to keep track of projects (some timers have multiple displays just for this purpose). If it gets really busy, I use masking tape or sticky notes for identification. Electronic digital timers are reliable and easy to set, but any quality timer will do. Some timers are designed to be worn around your neck or clip onto your clothes, and there are timers that function as a thermometer, too.

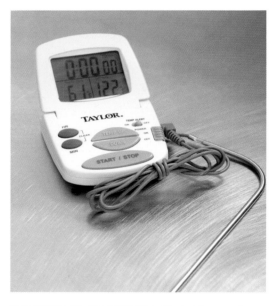

This digital probe thermometer with remote console also has a timer function.

Metal and plastic bench scrapers (top and middle) and a plastic bowl scraper (bottom)

Thermometers

Thermometers are important and every well-stocked kitchen should have one. I prefer to use a probe thermometer with a digital console, but any instant-read probe thermometer will do. It is indispensable when you need to check the temperature of liquid ingredients and dough as it is coming off the mixer. My recommendation: save yourself both some money and space and buy a timer/thermometer combination.

Scrapers

A bowl scraper is made from plastic and has a soft contour that hugs the curves of any bowl. This tool is very versatile; not only does it scrape dough from a bowl, but it also gently incorporates quick bread ingredients without developing too much gluten.

Bench scrapers are rectangular pieces of metal with wooden handles (but plastic versions exist, too) and are essential tools in the bakeshop. Use them to scrape sticky dough and flour off your work surface, or for dividing dough after the bulk fermentation stage.

Proofing Containers

Proofing containers are made of plastic and have lids. Clear plastic containers give an unobstructed view of the fermentation process. Plastic insulates during the proofing stage and protects the dough from any drastic changes in environmental temperature. Always choose a container that is large enough for the dough to comfortably double in size.

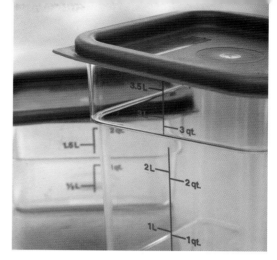

Plastic proofing containers help to insulate the dough while it is rising.

Mixing Bowls

Mixing bowls come in all different sizes and materials, including glass, stainless steel, and plastic. All work equally well for mixing, and you may choose one variety over the other for different applications. For example, I tend not to use glass bowls for the simple reason that they can break and easily contaminate a kitchen. Stainless-steel bowls are the most common found in professional kitchens; they are simple and durable and do not transfer any flavors from one product to another. Plastic and melamine bowls can be heated in the microwave, are easily cleaned, and do not react to any acidic ingredients. Since they do not conduct heat very well, they can also double as your proofing container if you cover the top with a plastic film during the fermentation cycle.

Plastic mixing bowls can double as proofing containers.

Mesh strainers strain liquids and sift dry ingredients.

Mesh Strainers/Sifters

These come in all different shapes and mesh sizes, and are used for straining liquids and sifting powdered ingredients, such as flours and powdered sugar.

A classic wooden rolling pin (right) and a wooden French tapered rolling pin (left) rest on top of a silicone French straight rolling pin (bottom).

Rolling Pins

A rolling pin is an iconic baking tool and is a must in every baking household. The two most common styles are the *classic rolling pin* and the *French rolling pin*.

The classic pin has a straight barrel with handles that extend beyond the main body. The heavier the rolling pin, the less energy you have to exert during the rolling process. Modern improvements, such as ball bearings, give a smoother rolling motion, but also make this type more prone to damage through repeated exposure to water.

The French rolling pin is a simple barrel without handles and comes in either a straight or tapered version. It is thinner than a classic pin and, due to the ergonomics, is most often used for more delicate work. The lack of handles limits the amount of pressure you can exert during the rolling process.

Colorful silicone versions of both styles can be found, too. A major benefit of its nonstick surface is that less flour is required during the process of rolling out the dough. As a result, the dough does not become excessively dry when rerolling the dough. The downside is the price: they usually cost up to twice as much as a wooden pin.

Scoops with trigger releases are one of the quickest ways to portion out batters, particularly for muffins.

Ice-Cream Scoops

Scoops with trigger releases are one of the quickest ways to portion out batters, particularly for muffins.

Wire cooling racks are essential for baking.

Cooling Racks

Racks allow adequate air to circulate around a cooling product. You can place the baking molds directly on top of the racks to prevent the buildup of moisture between the wall of the baking mold and the product during the cooling process.

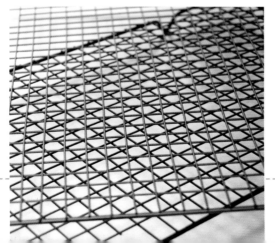

Spatulas

Rubber spatulas are great for keeping a distance between the baker and the batter. I recommend this tool for any application that is too stiff for a whisk to handle. It has been my experience that the rubber heads do not like to stick to wood, so I prefer using the ones with heavy-duty plastic handles. Some spatulas are heat resistant, and can be used for stovetop cooking.

Metal spatulas come in all different sizes and two different shapes: straight and offset. A straight spatula is used for icing cakes and the offset spatula is great for working on product that is placed directly on the work surface. Experiment with different sizes and angles to find the one you are most comfortable with. A smaller spatula will be better suited for detailed work and a larger one will efficiently cover more surface area.

Wheels

Pastry wheels come with either a straight or fluted metal blade that should be no larger than 2 inches (5 cm) in diameter for pastry applications (anything larger should be for deep-dish pizza, not croissants). The sharper the blade, the cleaner the cut. When the blade becomes too dull or the wheel wiggles, it is time to replace it and get a new pastry wheel.

A *multiwheel*, commonly used by professional bakers, is not for cutting; rather, for evenly dividing portions. It is used to mark out divisions on a sheet pan of brownies or dividing a sheet of Danish dough.

Look for a rubber spatula on a plastic handle.

Two different sizes of offset spatulas

A pastry wheel (top) and a multiwheel (bottom) perform different tasks: one cuts and the other measures.

Three essential knives (from top to bottom): a paring knife, a serrated knife, and a French knife

Choose a heavy-duty box grater for years of good use.

The Microplane has revolutionized the way we zest.

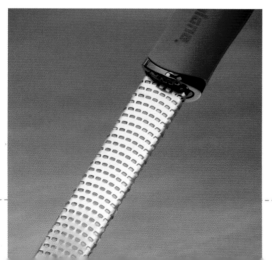

Knives

Knives are essential tools and choosing them can be daunting. You can get by with three basic types: a *paring knife*, a *French knife*, and a *serrated knife*. A paring knife has a tapered blade 3 to 4 inches (7.6 to 10.2 cm) long, and is mainly used for delicate trimming, peeling, and coring. The French knife, or chef's knife, can have a blade anywhere from 4 to 12 inches (10.2 to 30.5 cm) in length. The blade has a gentle curve designed to rock back and forth and lessen the strain of chopping. A serrated knife, with a blade 6 to 12 inches (15 to 30.5 cm) long, is perfect for cutting baked goods without damaging the fragile crumb structure.

Box Grater

A box grater is handy for many grating applications. A word to the wise: do not use the perforated surface to zest citrus fruits—more zest ends up stuck to the surface of the grater than in the formula. Use a Microplane instead.

Microplane

A Microplane is one of my favorite, all-time kitchen tools. Originally used in woodworking, this gem of a tool has literally revolutionized the use of zest in the kitchen. It takes only the outermost portion of the rind containing the pure essential citrus oils for use in the formulas. It also works great for hard cheeses, hard spices, chocolate, and more.

Pastry Brushes

Brushes are used to apply glazes, syrups, and washes to dough both before and after baking. When buying a brush with either natural or synthetic bristles, check that the bristles are well attached With a silicone brush, look for one that has thin silicone bristles around a flat central portion. It is good to have several brushes and dedicate at least one for savory flavors.

Treat your pastry brush well and hand wash the brush with warm water and mild detergent. Heat from the dishwasher will soften the glue adhering the bristles to the handlen and the brush will quickly deteriorate.

Even a simple thing like a pastry brush has not been spared the age of silicone. A silicone brush that has thin bristles surrounding a flat central portion allows the brush to hold on to the liquids better, but since silicone is inherently nonstick, I generally find these brushes less than ideal.

English Muffin Rings

These rings are highly specialized pieces of equipment designed for one purpose only: to encircle the dough on the pan while you make English muffins. They are not too expensive, but if you don't care to add yet another set of tools to your drawer, you can try using circle cutters, or rinse empty tuna fish cans and cut out both the tops and bottoms.

Circle and Biscuit Cutters

Round and scalloped round (biscuit) cutters can be bought as either individual cutters or in boxed, graduated sets. To prevent cutters from rusting, dust a bit of cornstarch over them before storing.

A natural bristle pastry brush (top) and a silicone pastry brush (bottom)

These rings are just for making English muffins.

A graduated set of circle cutters

CHAPTER THREE

Techniques

WHETHER THEY LOVE TO BAKE OR NOT, most people will agree that baking is an art form. Having had the personal experience of both attending art school and completing a European pastry apprenticeship, I can attest to that fact. The tenets of both fields are the same in two key ways: you must master the basics before anything else, and you must practice, practice, practice. Whether you consider yourself an artist in the studio or kitchen, it is critical to have a solid command of the fundamentals of your medium. It is far better to take the time (and struggle if necessary) to get it right at the beginning than to rush and gloss over techniques without truly mastering them; you will only pay for your haste later in the form of exasperation.

In my many years of teaching and working with students in the bakeshop, I have witnessed countless fledgling pastry chefs and bakers make their share of mistakes as they learn the fundamentals, some humorous, others downright frightening!

The good news is that mistakes are a necessary part of learning. After all, how are you supposed to know that you have whipped cream too far until you have actually done it? Or know what an overdeveloped dough actually feels like until you've kept one in the mixer too long? Chapter 3 teaches the basic techniques needed to successfully execute the recipes found later in the book. Starting with instruction on how to measure ingredients correctly, you'll then progress to learning the different mixing techniques. Quick bread techniques are simple and include rubbing, blending, and creaming methods. Yeasted bread techniques are slightly more complex and require more time, but the results are worth the effort. And, I share time-saving baking techniques that will help you make the most of the recipes in this book.

Remember: Do not be afraid of making mistakes. Just learn from them, and let the mastery begin!

Measuring

In the baking industry, a recipe is referred to as a formula. This may conjure up visions of beakers in a science lab, but baking is a science as well as an art. And just as the amount chemicals combined in a laboratory experiment need to be precise, the ingredients in a baking recipe must be carefully measured and combined in the appropriate proportions and sequence for the baking magic to properly take place.

Just as you did in chemistry class, you will learn to weigh your ingredients. Measuring by weight is a much more consistent and accurate way to measure ingredients than by volume, especially in baking. Stovetop cooking has a bit more flexibility with precision, in terms of exactness. You can't quite get away with cavalierly tossing fistfuls of baking ingredients into a mixing bowl.

As described in chapter 2, different styles of scales are available. It really doesn't matter which type you use; the process is essentially the same.

Measuring Ingredients with a Scale

- Place the scale on a flat, hard surface, and if it is digital, turn it on. If there is the option, select the unit of measure (grams or ounces). I recommend using grams.
- Place on the scale a bowl large enough to contain the ingredients to be weighed. Depending on the recipe and the order in which the ingredients are mixed, this can be the actual mixing bowl from your mixer (provided the scale can accommodate the weight of the bowl plus that of the ingredients).
- Zero or *tare* the scale. This subtracts the weight of what is on the scale (in this case, the bowl) so that only the weight of the ingredients will be weighed.

- Place the first ingredient in the bowl until the desired weight is achieved.
- If the recipe calls for several ingredients to be combined at the same time, they can all be consecutively scaled together into the same bowl. Simply zero/tare the scale again and continue weighing out the additional ingredients one at a time, making sure to zero/tare the scale between adding ingredients.
- **Hint:** Many times recipes call for wet ingredients to be combined first, with the dry ingredients added later. Usually I scale wet ingredients directly into the mixer bowl and scale the dry ingredients together into a separate bowl.

Measuring Ingredients with Measuring Cups and Spoons

If you do not own a scale and have no intention of purchasing one, then using a good set of quality measuring cups and spoons is your only option. To achieve the best results possible, follow these guidelines when measuring:

DRY OR STICKY INGREDIENTS

When measuring dry or sticky ingredients, such as flour, sugar, brown sugar, butter, and corn syrup, use a set of graduated nesting measuring cups (usually ranging from ¼ cup to 1 cup [57 to 227 g]). Dry ingredients can be scooped or spooned into the measuring cups and then leveled with a knife or straight edge of a spatula. Hard flours such as bread flour can usually just be scooped from the bin, whereas softer flours (those that clump together when squeezed) such as cake flour are best measured by spooning the flour into the cup. Granulated sugar is scooped and leveled, but brown sugar is scooped and packed before leveling. Butter and margarine are usually sold by the stick with measurements marked on the side, but if you have odd pieces left over or are using a block of butter, then you should use a spatula to press it into the measuring cups (making sure there are no air bubbles) and then level at the top with a straight edge. This is the same method to use with other solid-fat type ingredients, such as shortening and peanut butter.

Use the same approach when measuring small amounts of dry or sticky ingredients in measuring spoons. Measure over a bowl to catch any excess scraped off during leveling.

Lightly spraying the measuring cups with nonstick spray before measuring sticky ingredients such as honey, corn syrup, and sour cream will enable these ingredients to slip out of the cup easier.

LIQUID INGREDIENTS

Liquids such as water, milk, and oil should be measured in a liquid measuring cup if you are to measure greater than ¼ cup [55 ml]. (For any amount ¼ cup [55 ml] or less, use a graduated measuring cup or measuring spoons.) These are clear measuring cups made from either glass or plastic and usually have a pouring spout and handle. Place the cup on a flat, level surface and pour the liquid into the cup. When viewed from eye level, you will notice that the liquid curves up to meet the edge of the measuring cup. This curve is known as the *meniscus*. Do not measure from the top contact point, but rather from the bottom of the curve of the meniscus.

When measuring smaller amounts of liquids in measuring spoons, measure over a bowl or sink to catch any spills.

Now I ask you, with all of these different vessels to be cleaned between uses—why not just buy a scale?

CONSISTENCY Is the KEY

You will notice that every formula in this book has at least three categories of measuring: grams (metric weight), weight (standard units), and volume (cups). An additional column, baker's percentage, is added for yeasted breads. The original source of measurement for all formulas is grams, and it is listed as the first column. The second column is the direct conversion of the metric weight into the standard units. The third column gives measurements in spoons and cups—it is not intended to be a direct translation of weight; rather, to function independently as its own column. And the last column of baker's percentage is included as a courtesy to those bakers who like to use this system to frequently scale the formula yields either up or down.

The important point to be made is this: before measuring the ingredients of any formula, decide which measurement method you are going to use and then stick with it. For example, do not weigh your milk and eggs and then measure your flour in cups. You will have the greatest chance of success if you pick a column and then use only the measurements indicated

Quick Bread Techniques

Quick breads rise (or are leavened) through a chemical reaction that produces carbon dioxide (CO_2). Baked goods that contain baking powder and baking soda are classified as quick breads and include cakes, muffins, cookies, pancakes, and waffles. The mixing methods for quick breads minimize the dough's gluten development, creating a tender crumb structure (instead of building the dough's gluten structure).

There are three basic methods of mixing or incorporating ingredients together when making quick breads: rubbing, creaming, and blending, .

Rubbing ● DVD CONTENT

The rubbing method, also called the biscuit method, creates a soft dough suitable for gentle rolling and shaping. Biscuits, scones, and Irish soda bread are all quick breads that are made with the rubbing method.

As its name implies, the rubbing method involves rubbing or cutting fat into flour (similar to the method for making pie dough). The fat is dispersed throughout the dough, protecting the gluten strands from absorbing water, thereby reducing gluten development. When baked, the water held within the fat is turned into steam in the oven, resulting in a physical lift and creating a light and flaky product.

For the best results, the fat (unsalted butter is used throughout this book) should be as cold as possible. To prevent overmixing, it is best to use the fingers or a pastry blender to cut the fat into the flour; a food processor with a metal blade on pulse mode can also yield good results. You can use a mixer with a paddle attachment on a very low speed, as long as it is mixed carefully under a watchful eye.

After cutting in the fat, the liquid ingredients, such as eggs and milk or water, are added. Again, it is best if these ingredients are cold. The dough is mixed just until everything is incorporated; fat particles will still be evident in the dough. Recipes will often call for additional ingredients such as dried fruits, nuts, or chocolate chunks. These are added to the dough at various stages of the mixing process.

The soft dough is removed from the mixing bowl and gently folded five to seven times on a floured surface. This gentle motion creates even layers within the dough but does not overdevelop the gluten. The top of the dough is dusted with a bit of flour and a rolling pin is used to roll out the dough to a uniform thickness. Turn over the dough and alternate the rolling direction to avoid any shape distortion during final baking. Use a sharp knife or cutter to cut out the dough shapes, and place the dough on a parchment-lined sheet pan or nonstick cookie sheet. Let the dough rest for 20 to 30 minutes before baking to allow the gluten to relax so that no shape distortion is evident after baking.

THE RUBBING METHOD

a) **Sift the flour** into a bowl.

b) **Cut the fat** into the flour by hand (or with a pastry blender).

c) **Make a well** in the flour mixture. Pour the egg mixture into the well.

d) **Mix the dough** together by hand.

e) **Fold the dough** several times on a floured surface.

f) **Cut the dough** into shapes with a sharp knife (or cutter).

Creaming DVD CONTENT

This mixing method produces a cakelike texture by incorporating solid fats at room temperature (such as butter) with crystalline sugar (such as granulated or brown sugar.) The sugar and fat are creamed together on medium speed using a mixer's paddle attachment. As air cells are formed and captured in the batter, a light color and texture is achieved. During mixing, periodically scrape down the sides of the bowl and attachment to ensure all ingredients are uniformly mixed.

When the mixture is pale in color, the room temperature eggs are added slowly. In general, solid fats (such as butter) and liquids (such as eggs) are difficult to bind. Thankfully, eggs contain a natural emulsifier called lecithin, which in this case helps bind the eggs to the butter and allow the fat particles to be more evenly dispersed throughout the batter, yielding a more tender, better-textured result.

It is important that the butter and the eggs be at room temperature (65° to 70°F, or 18° to 21°C) and that the eggs are added slowly, allowing the lecithin to do its job. You can either add each whole egg one at a time, mixing thoroughly between eggs, or you can whisk all the eggs together in a separate bowl, and then slowly stream them into the creamed butter in three or four stages. Again, scrape down the sides of the bowl and attachment as necessary.

If the process is rushed, separation between the eggs (liquids) and butter (solids) can occur. Similarly, if the eggs are too cold when coming in contact with the butter, the butter will "seize up" and start to separate from the eggs.

CORRECTING SEIZED BUTTER

If your butter seizes during mixing, you can sometimes remedy the situation by taking the mixing bowl off the mixer and gently warming the bottom over a gas stove burner to raise the temperature (or you could try the heat from a hairdryer in a pinch). If the separation continues, do not throw out the batter! The formula will still work and taste fine; it just won't develop the same level of volume during baking.

a) **Mix the butter and sugar** until pale in color.

b) **Slowly add the egg mixture** (at room temperature).

c) **Add the dry ingredients** slowly, just until incorporated.

Blending ⬤ DVD CONTENT

The blending method is the simplest of the three methods and is only used when a quick bread recipe calls for liquid fats, such as oil. All dry ingredients, except the sugars, are combined and set aside. The oil, eggs, and sugar are then blended with a whisk. The dry ingredients are added to the egg mixture and mixed either by hand or in a mixer at low speed until just incorporated. Additional ingredients may be called for, such as water or other liquids, and are added accordingly. Dried fruits, nuts, berries, chocolate chips, or other flavorful additions are gently folded in at the end of the mixing.

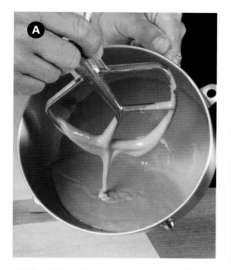

a) **Blend the oil**, eggs, and sugar together.

b) **Add the dry ingredients** to the liquid mixture and blend.

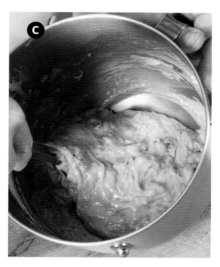

c) **The batter is mixed** and ready to pour or scoop into forms.

TUNNELING

What happens to a quick bread dough or batter when it has been overmixed? For one, the gluten strands build strength and develop more than they should. This results in a tougher, chewier product. Sometimes the gluten develops so much strength that it is able to capture the carbon dioxide released during the chemical leavening process. As the gas is trapped, air pockets balloon up inside of the product and create holes. This characteristic is known to professional bakers as tunneling.

If even after paying careful attention to the mixing times your products still show signs of tunneling, you can try replacing up to 20 percent of the all-purpose flour called for in the recipe with pastry flour. Pastry flour contains less gluten-building protein than all-purpose flour, and using a mixture of the different flours should alleviate the tunneling problem.

Yeasted Dough Techniques

Whereas quick breads get their rising power through chemical leaveners, yeasted products achieve volume through the natural fermentation of yeast. Yeast is a single celled organism that feeds from the simple sugars naturally present in flour. Fermentation takes place in the presence of warmth (ideally 75° to 78°F [24° to 26°C) and moisture and accelerates with higher temperature. It is a complicated process in which the starches in the flour are broken down into simple sugars, which then act as food for the yeast. The yeast "eats" the sugar, giving off carbon dioxide and alcohol in the process. These molecules of carbon dioxide form bubbles of gas that are trapped by the gluten matrix in the dough, creating a balloon around the carbon dioxide. The feeding cycle continues until either the yeast runs out of sugar or the bread is baked.

A skilled baker strives to enhance the flavor and aroma of the bread by controlling this process of fermentation. Success lies in part with the mastery of some basic fundamentals and techniques:

Pre-ferments

A relatively easy way to increase flavor without having to increase the overall fermentation of a final dough is to utilize *pre-ferments*. A pre-ferment is a specified combination of flour, water, and instant yeast and is mixed prior to preparing the final dough. The pre-ferment is stored in a controlled manner, either cold or at room temperature, depending on the flavor profile desired. A cold-stored pre-ferment assumes an acidic flavor profile (like lemon juice or vinegar), whereas a room temperature stored pre-ferment develops a lactic flavor profile (comparable to yogurt). It is then mixed into the final dough, where it helps to build flavor, strength, and increased shelf life.

Sourdough starters are a special kind of pre-ferment that maintains the growth of wild yeast cultures; they need special care and feeding to ensure consistent leavening activity. The pre-ferments utilized in this book are made with commercially manufactured instant yeast and are specifically mixed and used up in one application.

There are four main types of commercially leavened pre-ferments:

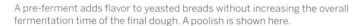

A pre-ferment adds flavor to yeasted breads without increasing the overall fermentation time of the final dough. A poolish is shown here.

POOLISH

A *poolish* contributes a sweet, nutty, and slightly lactic flavor profile and imparts a very extensible strength attribute to breads. It is made with a one-to-one ratio of water (or other type of liquid, such as milk) to flour, making it the wettest of all the pre-ferments. It is traditionally made the day before baking by first placing the water in a mixing bowl, followed by the flour and yeast. Mix the ingredients together with a spatula until you have achieved a smooth consistency. Place the poolish in a plastic container that will allow it to double in size and cover it with a lid or plastic wrap. Let it ferment at room temperature until it has matured; it will have a nice balance of large air bubbles and smaller indentations on the top surface. If you notice a "high water mark" on the sides of the container, then the poolish has over-fermented and will not properly contribute to the fermentation of the final dough. A poolish should never be kept for more than 24 hours.

BIGA

A *biga* is much firmer than a poolish and adds an acidic flavor profile along with ample strength-building characteristics to bread. It was originally developed in Italy to strengthen the lower gluten-forming flours traditionally found in the region. While this stiffer pre-ferment can be mixed by hand, it is far easier and better to use a stand mixer. Mix the water (or other type of liquid, such as milk), flour, and instant yeast together into a smooth mass, making sure there are no dry spots in the dough. Spray a plastic container with nonstick cooking spray. Lightly press the biga upside down into the container and then turn it over so that the top has a light coating of oil on it. This keeps the surface soft and supple and prevents it from cracking as it expands. Cover with a lid or plastic wrap and let it ferment at room temperature. Traditionally, a biga is mixed at room temperature and then placed in a cool environment, like a basement, for 24 to 48 hours. However, in today's modern baking world, many bakers split the time of fermentation, keeping the pre-ferment at room temperature for a few hours and then placing it in the refrigerator. A perfectly matured biga will double in size and has a strong fermented odor. If a piece is torn off, small air cells are visible within the dough.

SPONGE

A sponge pre-ferment is often used with enriched doughs and has a consistency similar to a biga. Since a sponge contains no sugars or fats, it gives the yeast a chance to jump-start the fermentation process and build some gluten strength before the mixing of the final dough. Enriched doughs contain sugar and/or fat, which tenderizes the dough by interfering with the formation of the gluten, so the extra strength built up in the sponge is a welcome addition to the final dough. It is mixed and handled in the same manner as a biga, but traditionally is allowed to ferment for only 2 to 4 hours (even though in some instances it can be left overnight).

PÂTE FERMENTÉE

Also known as "old dough," this is the only type of pre-ferment that is mixed to a full gluten development. After a dough is mixed and allowed to go through its bulk fermentation, some of it is removed, placed in a container, covered, and refrigerated overnight. The following day this pre-ferment is incorporated into the next batch of dough during the last few minutes of mixing on medium speed. It adds strength to the dough and imparts an acidic flavor profile due to its cold storage. Bakeries with fixed production schedules that bake the same bread daily can easily take advantage of this pre-ferment, but unless you are in the habit of making the same bread every day at home, the pâte fermentée is difficult to utilize.

Mixing

The first step in developing a bread dough is to mix the ingredients together. This is preferably accomplished in a stand mixer, but can also be done by hand if you are both ambitious and patient (and strong arm muscles don't hurt, either). Some people like to mix their dough in a food processor. Although these specific formulas have not been tested with this method, nothing is stopping you from giving it a try. Charlie Van Over's *The Best Bread Ever* is a comprehensive book to making bread using a food processor and I recommend using it as a resource if you are particularly interested in this technique.

Mixing a yeasted dough in a stand mixer conveniently produces a good dough with little physical effort.

Mixing Fundamentals

⊙ DVD CONTENT

I find it most helpful to weigh out the amount of water called for in the formula and place it first in the bowl of the mixer. This is to help prevent (or at least lessen the amount of) dough from sticking to the sides of the bowl during the mixing. After scaling and adding the water (or other liquid), you can continue with the formula instructions by adding the next batch of ingredients. These will depend on the bread you are making. A simple lean dough would include the additional ingredients of flour, yeast, and salt. Scale out these ingredients and place them in the mixing bowl. Then, using a dough hook attachment, turn the mixer on at a low speed to slowly incorporate the ingredients together. Within 1 to 2 minutes, the dough will reach what is called a "shaggy mass" stage. The ingredients begin to clump together with an unstructured and somewhat rough texture; it almost forms a ball in the mixer, but not quite. Continue mixing at low speed until you have a homogeneous blend. Increase the mixing speed to a medium speed and continue mixing until the dough comes together to form a more cohesive unit and none of the dough is sticking to the sides of the mixer. This is known to bakers as the "cleanup stage" or the "pickup stage" since the dough is cleaned up (or picked up) from the sides of the mixer. (As always, there can be exceptions to the rule—the gibassier dough, for example, is still too soft to form a tight ball and a clean mixer.)

At this point, you want to test the gluten development within the dough. To do this, remove a small piece of dough and use moist or wet fingers to coax the dough into a "window." The smoother and more well developed the dough is, the thinner and larger of a gluten window you will be able to pull without it breaking or tearing. Sometimes you want a very well-developed dough with a strong gluten structure and sometimes you want to remove the dough from the mixer before it gets to that point. It all depends on the type of bread to be made. Each formula will indicate how developed a dough should be before removing it from the mixer.

a) **A dough mixed** to the "shaggy mass" stage

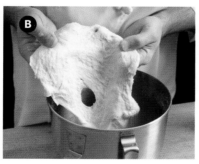

b) **A window test** on an underdeveloped dough

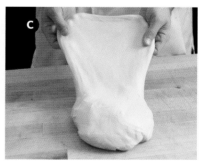

c) **A window test** on a fully developed dough

Hand Mixing ● DVD CONTENT

If you do not own a stand mixer and are developing a dough by hand, you will need more time and physical stamina than when mixing with a stand mixer. Hand mixing methods vary from baker to baker and each has his or her individual style and preference. When mixing by hand, I like to start with the dry ingredients scaled out into a bowl. I then make a well in the center of the dry ingredients and pour in the wet ingredients. I prefer to use a plastic scraper to work the wet and dry ingredients together, scraping the outside of the bowl and using a motion that moves up and then over toward the middle. Once the dough reaches the "shaggy mass" stage, I turn it out onto a wooden work surface to continue the mixing. Most people refer to this as "kneading" the dough, but essentially it is accomplishing the same task that a stand mixer does during the mixing process; that is, incorporating the ingredients and building the gluten strength in the dough. Taking the mass of dough, I use the heel of my dominant hand (in my case, my right hand) and press along the top surface of the dough to stretch it out forward. I use my left hand on the side of the dough as a guide. Then I cup the fingers of my right hand under the top edge of the dough and curl it under as I pull the dough back, turning the dough slightly with the motion. This entire process is repeated until the dough has developed to the stage desired.

a) **Form a well** in the center of the dry ingredients and add the liquids ingredients.

b) **Use a bowl scraper** to gently incorporate the ingredients together.

c) **Turn out the dough** onto a lightly floured surface and begin to knead.

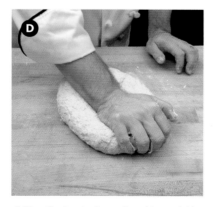

d) **Use the heel of your hand** to push the dough down and away from you.

e) **Use your fingers** to roll the dough back on top, turning the dough slightly.

Temperature

You will notice that the yeasted dough formulas all indicate a starting temperature for the water in the ingredients. Getting the liquid to the right temperature before mixing will aid in getting the dough to reach the ideal temperature as it comes off the mixer. In certain situations you may need to deviate from the given temperatures to help offset the temperature in a cold room or if you are baking without air conditioning during the heat of the summer (see "The Friction Factor" below.)

In the baker's perfect world, the temperature of the dough should be between 75° and 78°F (24° and 26°C) when it is removed from the mixer. This is the optimum temperature for fermentation to occur. The temperature should be measured with either a digital or standard probe thermometer. In this case, using an infrared thermometer has one major disadvantage: it only measures the outside surface of the dough. Since the surface temperature will be cooler than the interior of the dough, it will only be accurate for the first few minutes of the fermentation process. Sometimes the dough is not within the optimum

The ideal temperature of a dough after mixing is 75° to 78°F (24° to 26°C).

range, and there are a few steps you can take to remedy the situation. If the dough is below 75°F (26°C), then you can help move things along by placing the dough in a warmer spot, for example near a sunny window or in the oven with the light on. If the dough is much warmer, be prepared for the dough to "move" or rise faster than the timing indicated in the formulas.

Sometimes it is possible to cool the dough off by spreading it out on a marble slab; the coolness of the stone will absorb some of the excess heat within the dough, thereby lowering the overall dough temperature. Or, if space allows, you can place the dough in its container in the refrigerator for a short amount of time.

THE FRICTION FACTOR

Some professional bakers utilize a complex formula that computes the water temperature, flour temperature, room temperature, and what is known as the "friction factor" (a number based on the heat produced through friction during the mixing that varies with the type of mixer being used) to determine the length of mixing time. It requires a very controlled and scientific approach to mixing dough.

Personally, I prefer to adjust only the temperature of the water (it's easy to make the water from a faucet hotter or colder) and figure that both the flour and the room are constants at room temperature (68° to 72°F [20° to 22°C]). I then rely on a gluten window test, along with my experience and "finger feel," to tell me when the dough is ready to remove from the mixer. If a room is particularly hot or cold, I take that into consideration and will adjust the temperature of the water to compensate. In the end, proper gluten development trumps temperature; if the gluten development seems right but the dough is not within the ideal temperature range, I make adjustments in bulk fermentation times.

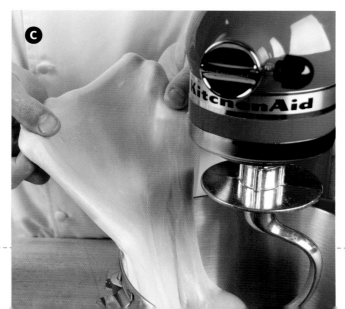

Mixing an Enriched Dough ● DVD CONTENT

Many of the yeasted formulas in this book are enriched doughs, meaning that they have some type of fat-enriched ingredient incorporated into them, such as butter, oil, or eggs. This is where the mixing can get tricky without the use of a mixer. Fat acts as a tenderizer by coating the protein and slowing down the formation of gluten. The tricky part is incorporating the fat into the dough while still allowing enough strength-building gluten to form, to allow proper shaping and development of the dough. An enriched dough needs to be mixed for a minimum of 10 minutes and sometimes up to 20 minutes, depending on the mixer. But wait, it gets even trickier! The process of the dough hook mixing the dough produces heat through friction. With shorter mixing times this is not an issue, but with an enriched dough, the long and vigorous mixing sessions can very easily increase the dough temperature to above and beyond the ideal range. To make matters worse, the melting point of butter starts at 82°F (28°C). This means that if the temperature of a dough enriched with butter exceeds this level during mixing, the butter in the dough will start to melt and actually leak out of the dough.

It may sound as if the odds are stacked against ever developing a decent enriched dough that will yield a tender, delicate product. Have faith; if you follow the guidelines and are mindful of the temperature ranges, you should have no problem achieving good results. They may not be perfect with the first attempt, but the following tips will help you develop the confidence to tackle enriched doughs head-on.

(a) **Prior to mixing** an enriched dough, soften the butter with a rolling pin.

(b) **Slowly incorporate** the butter into the dough in stages.

(c) **Continue to mix** the dough until it is fully developed and has a nice gluten window.

First, **make sure all of your ingredients are cold**, particularly the liquid ingredients and the butter. In a very warm environment, some bakers also chill down their flour and mixing bowl as well, but this is usually not necessary in most circumstances.

Scale the liquids (usually milk and eggs) into the mixing bowl and then add the dry ingredients (such as flour, salt, instant yeast, and sugar) to the bowl. Mix these together at a low speed until the cleanup stage.

While the dough is mixing in this first stage, **make the butter to be added to the dough soft and pliable**. Do this by using a rolling pin to pound the butter until you achieve a play-dough-like consistency. Do not confuse this pliable butter with the softened butter you have at room temperature. The butter will still be cold, just more plastic than before. This allows a smoother and easier incorporation into the dough.

Once you have achieved a plastic, pliable butter and your dough has reached the cleanup stage, **increase the mixing speed to medium** and start to add the butter in small (about one quarter of the total) increments. After you add the first part of butter, **continue mixing at medium speed** until it is completely incorporated into the dough. You can usually tell this by the sound that the dough makes as it works its way around the mixer.

When the butter is first added, you will hear a sticky, slapping noise as the butter is churned into the dough. As you continue mixing, the butter will homogenize into the dough, the slapping sound will subside, and the sides of the mixer will be clean and free of butter and dough residue. Continue the same process for each addition of butter, making sure that each part is fully incorporated before adding the next.

After all of the butter has been completely incorporated, the mixing continues until a nice window can be formed during a gluten window test. Depending on the efficiency of the mixer,

this can take anywhere from 10 to 20 minutes of total mixing time. Keep an eye on the temperature of the dough as it comes off the mixer—the temperature could creep up to 82°F (28°C); much beyond that and the butter that you worked so hard to carefully incorporate may start to leak out of the dough. If the temperature reaches this point, place the mixing bowl in the refrigerator for a few minutes.

Mixing in Fruit, Nuts, and Seeds ⊙ DVD CONTENT

One way a baker adds variety, flavor, and texture to breads is through the addition of such ingredients as fruit and nuts. These are commonly added to the dough at the end stages of mixing after the dough has developed a good gluten structure. This gluten structure captures the chunks of fruit and nuts and creates a nice membrane layer over them during the later phase of shaping.

Add any fruit, seeds, or nuts at the end stages of mixing an enriched dough.

Shaping ⦿ DVD CONTENT

After the dough has been mixed to the desired stage of gluten development (and this will vary from dough to dough), the dough needs to be shaped. This is usually done in two stages: *preshaping* and *final shaping*. With the enriched doughs in this book, the long, intense mixing process develops much of the dough's strength and coupled with the fact that most breakfast breads rely on baking forms to create their shape, the additional manipulation of a final shaping is often unnecessary.

In the preshaping stage, the baker manipulates the dough into a form similar to the final shape of the dough, in effect "training" the dough for its final shape. Most of the breads in this book require a preshaping or final shaping into a round. Some additional techniques are required to make specially shaped breads, such as gibassier and stollen, and will be covered in their respective formulas. The motions required for both preshaping and final shaping are essentially the same, with the final shaping process creating a tighter and more finished form. There are two different approaches to creating the rounds, both of which achieve the same results.

Preshaping/Shaping a Round, version 1

Take a unit of dough and gently cup one or two hands (depending on the size of the dough) over the dough, letting your fingers relax and drape over the dough. Use a small circular motion to move the dough around on the work surface and coax it into a ball-like shape. As you move the dough, press the heel of your hand gently into the dough as you circle away from you and then use your fingers to pull the dough back toward you. Continue this motion until the dough starts to feel tight, but take care not to overwork the dough. Depending on the product, the preshaped rounds are either placed in baking forms or on a wooden surface and loosely covered with plastic wrap to rest before final shaping. Before final shaping, gently compress the dough to expel excess gas.

(a) Preshaping small rounds

Preshaping/Shaping a Round, version 2

Leaving your pinkie finger and edge of hand in contact with the work surface, cup your hands around the back of the dough and coax it forward and clockwise. As the front edge of the dough creeps underneath itself, the outer membrane of the dough will start to tighten. Reposition your hands and keep repeating the motion until you have a nice, smooth surface. The round is now ready to be placed in a baking form or then rested and developed further.

Shaping a small round step-by-step

Shaping a larger unit of dough into a round

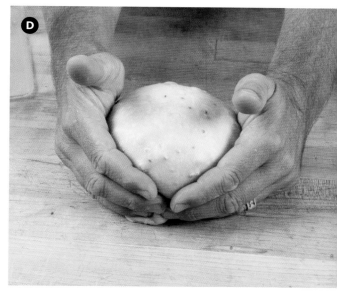

(a) **Cup your hands** or fingers around the back of the dough and coax it forward.

(b) **Gently lift the dough** turning clockwise ever so slightly.

(c) **Reposition your hands** and repeat the process until the dough membrane tightens into a smooth surface.

(d) **Use the same process** and motions to shape a larger unit of dough into a round.

Proofing and Retarding

Proofing happens after final shaping; it is the stage in which the dough has its final rise before baking. Ideally, the dough proofs in a protected environment (no drafts) at 75° to 78°F (24° to 26°C). The dough is still fermenting, but not as quickly as it was in the beginning fermentation stages just after mixing. An experienced baker can judge the stage of the proofing cycle through sight and feel. A good test is to make an indentation in the dough with a finger; the dough should push back slowly, but never recovers completely. Ideally the dough would reach about 85 percent of its full capacity during the proofing stage.

Retarding refers to the purposeful slowing down of the fermentation process. The baker achieves this by placing the dough in a controlled, cool environment such as a refrigerator. Sometimes the formula calls for retarding to develop a particular flavor, and other times it is done out of necessity: you have three trays of breads ready to bake and only two oven racks to bake them on . . . so one gets retarded in the refrigerator (covered, of course) until the oven space is free.

Lamination

Lamination is a special layering technique that bakers use to make certain types of breads and pastries, such as croissants and Danishes. The technique is made up of several processes. First, a layer of fat is created and sandwiched between two layers of dough. Then this package goes through a series of rolling and folding sequences. By doing so, each time the dough is rolled and folded, it increases the number of layers. This process also builds the gluten development and creates strength in the dough. These products actually have two sources of leavening agents: the yeast in the dough and the moisture content in the butter (remember, butter is 80 to 84 percent fat and the remainder is mostly water). When the products are baked, not only is the yeast working, but the water in the butter evaporates and expands the space between the layers as it tries to escape. This creates the lift between the layers and produces the nice flaky texture so desired in these types of breads and pastries. Since this technique is applicable to very specific products, a complete overview of the processes involved is covered in chapter 6.

Stacked chocolate and all-purpose laminated doughs; notice the striated layers of dough and butter.

Time-Saving Techniques

Between balancing work schedules and family commitments, it may be difficult to carve out space in the day for anything more than what is on your plate already, including baking. Luckily, there are some simple time-saving measures that will allow you to more readily enjoy breads and pastries hot from the oven.

Prescaling Ingredients

One of the easiest things you can do to save time is to prescale the ingredients. Set aside an hour to measure out the dry ingredients for your favorite recipes and place them in a plastic storage bag, making sure to label them with the formula and the date. Store them in the refrigerator if you plan to use them within the week, otherwise they can be stored in the freezer.

If you are making a yeasted product, wrap the yeast up separately in a bit of plastic wrap to keep it out of contact with the salt. Then place this little yeast package into the bag with the other dry ingredients and store. When you are ready to bake, much of the measuring has already been done. Just scale out the wet and other ingredients, and you are good to go!

Bake and Freeze

Baking a bit extra requires little more than the additional time in baking, and sometimes not even that, depending on the capacity of your oven and the kind of product you are making. (Check the capacity of your mixer before increasing the volume you intend to make.)

After baking, cool the product completely before storing to freeze. Wrap loaves and larger breads tightly in plastic wrap and either place in a freezer bag or then wrap again in aluminum foil. Remove as much air as possible from the bag. Muffins can be stored together in a plastic freezer bag; to prevent them from sticking together, prefreeze them directly in the muffin cups before putting into the freezer bag. When you are ready to eat the muffins, just remove and thaw to room temperature, or preheat the oven to 350°F (180°C, gas mark 4) and bake for 5 or 10 minutes until hot. Loaves can be reheated, too, but care needs to be taken to ensure that they don't dry out or burn. A lower baking temperature and an aluminum foil wrap can do the trick.

Par-Baking

This technique stands for "partial bake" and is utilized in many large commercial bakeries. Essentially a product is baked until it is about 80 percent done and the structure of the bread is set, then it is rapidly cooled down and frozen. When it is time to bake, the product is placed in a hot oven for 10 to 15 minutes to finish off the baking process. The product takes on its full color and crust development, but nothing more happens since the yeast was killed in the first bake and the starches were gelatinized and set.

In general, par-baking quick breads really doesn't make too much sense; they are so quick to mix and bake in the first place. The exception to this is scones. Scones do very well when mixed, shaped, and then frozen on a sheet pan prior to baking (do not egg wash the scones). Once frozen, you can consolidate in plastic freezer bags and depending on your freezer conditions, the dough can be kept for 1 to 2 weeks. The night before baking, place the scones in the refrigerator to defrost. The next day, simply egg-wash the surface and bake as directed. You will notice that the scones will not rise as much during the bake as those that are baked fresh, but there is barely a noticeable difference in flavor.

PART TWO

Baking

NOW THAT YOU ARE FULLY VERSED IN THE BASICS, it's time to roll up your sleeves and get baking! The process of baking involves all senses—aromas that fill the kitchen, the feel of the dough, sounds of flaky croissant layers being pulled apart, the tempting sight of muffins cooling on a rack, and of course, the mouth-watering taste as you enjoy your creation.

The pages that follow present easy recipes first that yield satisfying treats in practically no time, such as Mixed-Berry Muffins, Cranberry-Orange Scones, and the trusted Banana Muffins in chapter 4. If you have a little more time and are up for more of a challenge or have a more complete breakfast buffet in mind, move on to the traditional breakfast breads, such as Rum-Raisin-Almond Brioche, Pecan Sticky Buns, and Croissants in chapters 5 and 6. Above all, have fun and enjoy!

CHAPTER FOUR

Quick Breads, Muffins, and Scones

SIMPLE INGREDIENTS AND PREPARA-TION MAKE QUICK BREADS a welcoming first step into the world of baking. They are the perfect vehicle for introducing novice bakers to the methods of rubbing and blending, which can be done by hand, and creaming, an easy procedure for the mixer. The term *quick bread* refers to any baked product that uses chemical leaveners as its leavening agent. Remember that in baking a chemical leavener refers to baking powder and baking soda, not some dangerous concoction of laboratory chemicals. Not only do products like banana bread and zucchini bread fall into this category, but muffins, scones, and biscuits do as well (even cookies and cakes are technically part of this group).

This category of baking is extremely versatile, from the comforting and wholesome combinations of bran and raisins, to the sweeter side of hazelnuts and chocolate, to the savory flavors of caramelized onions and bacon, there is a quick bread for all tastes.

A basic scone recipe can easily transform from one group of ingredients to another. For example, the Cranberry-Orange Scone makes use of a much-loved flavor combination, but there is nothing to stop you from substituting other dried fruits for the cranberries, or replacing the cranberries with dark chocolate chunks to create a Chocolate-Orange Scone. What about a Chocolate-Cherry Scone? Just leave out the grated orange rind, and combine dried cherries and dark chocolate chunks to substitute for the cranberries. Dried blueberries, raisins, dates—almost any dried fruit will work. Let your culinary imagination run wild!

The same can be said for muffins and quick breads. Add chunks of dried apples to the bran muffin, for instance, instead of raisins, or create tropical banana bread with mango and candied pineapple or coconut instead of chocolate chunks. Try toasted nuts and seeds. Don't be afraid to experiment with flavors. You won't always hit the perfect combo immediately, but with some time and tweaking, you will develop your own original quick bread.

Cranberry-Orange Scones

YIELD:	**16 wedge scones or 14 round scones (3" [7.6 cm] diameter)**
BAKING TEMPERATURE:	**350°F (180°C, gas mark 4) convection mode**
BAKING TIME:	**15 to 18 minutes**

Scones are a traditional breakfast quick bread, similar to the American biscuit, and are believed to have originated in Scotland. While scones are easy to make, the soft and sticky dough takes some getting used to handling. You may be tempted to use an electric mixer, but do not be misled: for scones, mixing by hand trumps all other methods! The tartness of cranberry paired with the citrus tones of the orange zest is the perfect combination to wake up your taste buds in the morning. They are best served warm and enjoyed fresh, as they tend to dry out quickly.

Procedure:

1. Preheat a convection oven to 350°F (180°C, gas mark 4) for about 30 minutes before baking.

2. In a large mixing bowl, sift together all-purpose flour, granulated sugar, salt, and baking powder **(a)**.

3. Be sure the butter is cold and slice into small cubes (approximately 1 tablespoon [14 g] each). Work the butter into the dry ingredients using your fingertips until the butter pieces are no larger than the size of a pea. See Rubbing, page 50 **(b)**.

4. In a separate bowl, whisk together the eggs and buttermilk.

5. Make a depression in the center of the crumbly dry ingredients and pour the liquid ingredients into this well. Using a rubber spatula or a plastic dough scraper, blend the two together by folding the dry ingredients into the wet ingredients **(c, d)**.

6. When the batter just comes together and is still a little lumpy, add the dried cranberries and orange zest and hand mix briefly **(e)**.

Ingredient	Metric	Weight	Volume
All-purpose flour	440 g	15.5 oz	3½ cups
Granulated sugar	55 g	1.9 oz	¼ cup
Salt	4 g	0.1 oz	½ tsp
Baking powder	24 g	0.84 oz	2 tbsp
Unsweetened butter	148 g	5.2 oz	10 tbsp
Eggs, whole	82 g	2.9 oz	1 egg + 1 egg white*
Buttermilk	231 g	8.1 oz	1 cup
Dried cranberries	110 g	3.8 oz	1 cup
Orange zest	Zest from ½ orange	Zest from ½ orange	Zest from ½ orange
Egg Wash (page 152)	1 batch	1 batch	1 batch
Sanding sugar (optional)	As needed	As needed	As needed

* You can reserve the egg yolk to make an egg wash.

7. Place batter on a flour-dusted surface and fold together using your hands until the batter is manageable. However, do not overwork the batter. You will know if you did if your scones end up distorted and tough **(f)**.

8. Divide the dough in half and shape into balls. Press or roll into two ⅝" (1.6 cm) -thick disks. Cut each disk into triangular wedges, 8 per circle **(g)**.

Place scones on a parchment-lined half sheet pan or cookie sheet and let rest for 30 minutes. Brush the tops with an egg wash and sprinkle with sanding sugar or coarse granulated sugar **(h, i)**.

9. Bake in the preheated convection oven for approximately 15 to 18 minutes until golden brown on top. Remove from the oven and let cool on the sheet pan or cookie sheet. (You can place the scones on a wire rack to cool if you need to reuse the sheet pan.)

a) **Sift** the dry ingredients into a bowl.

b) **Cut the butter** into the flour mixture using your hands (or pastry blender).

c) **Pour the egg** mixture into a well in the dry ingredients.

d) **Blend the ingredients** together by hand.

e) **Add the dried fruit** and zest and blend by hand.

f) **Place dough** on a floured surface and fold together.

g) **Use a sharp knife** to cut the dough into wedges.

h) **Brush the tops** with an egg wash.

i) **Sprinkle** with sugar.

Ginger Scones

YIELD: **14 round scones or (3" [7.6 cm] diameter)**

BAKING TEMPERATURE: **350°F (180°C, gas mark 4) convection mode**

BAKING TIME: **15 to 18 minutes**

Ginger is a spice derived from the root of the ginger plant native to Southeast Asia. It can be bought whole, pickled, dried, ground, or in this case, candied. Candied ginger provides the perfect combination of warmth and sweetness to dress up a basic scone, while being moist and tender enough to add a nice texture, too. Herbalists recognize its ability to heal and soothe, while culinarians capitalize on its distinct strong flavor in a full range of dishes, from appetizers to entrées to desserts—ginger even finds its way into beverages and cocktails.

Ingredient	Metric	Weight	Volume
All-purpose* or bread flour	440 g	15.5 oz	3½ cups
Granulated sugar	55 g	1.9 oz	¼ cup
Salt	4 g	0.1 oz	½ tsp
Baking powder	18 g	0.63 oz	2 tbsp
Unsweetened butter	148 g	5.2 oz	10 tbsp
Eggs, whole	82 g	2.9 oz	1 egg + 1 egg white**
Buttermilk	231 g	8.1 oz	1 cup
Candied ginger	110 g	3.8 oz	1 cup
Egg Wash (page 152)	1 batch	1 batch	1 batch
Crumb Topping (optional, page 151)	1 batch	1 batch	1 batch

*When using all-purpose flour, remember to hold back a bit of liquid.

**You can reserve the egg yolk to make an egg wash.

Procedure:

1. Preheat a convection oven to 350°F (180°C, gas mark 4).

2. In a large mixing bowl, sift together the flour, granulated sugar, salt, and baking powder.

3. Slice the cold butter into small cubes (approximately 1 tablespoon [14 g] each). Using your fingertips, work the butter into the dry ingredients until the butter pieces are no larger than a pea (see Rubbing, page 50).

4. In a separate bowl, whisk together the eggs and buttermilk.

5. Make a depression in the center of the crumbly dry ingredients and pour the liquid ingredients into this well.

6. Using a rubber spatula or a plastic dough scraper, blend the two together by folding the dry ingredients into the wet ingredients.

7. When the batter just comes together and is still a little lumpy, add the candied ginger and hand mix briefly.

8. Place the batter on a flour-dusted surface and fold together using your hands, until the batter is manageable. Do not overwork the batter.

9. Shape into a large ball. Press down or roll until ⅝ inch (1.6 cm) thick. Using a 3-inch (7.6 cm) biscuit or circle cutter, cut out rounds. Gently fold the excess dough together and press down or roll out again to continue cutting out shapes **(a, b)**.

10. Place the scones on a parchment-lined half sheet pan or cookie sheet and let rest for 30 minutes.

11. Brush with egg wash. If desired, prepare Crumb Topping (see page 151) and sprinkle on top before baking (optional). Bake in the preheated convection oven for 15 to 18 minutes, until golden brown on top. Remove from the oven and let cool on the sheet pan or cookie sheet. You can place the scones on a wire rack to cool if you need to reuse the sheet pan **(c)**.

The ABCs of BUTTERMILK

The word "buttermilk" may conjure up images of a decadent full-fat cream, but you may be surprised to learn that there is no butter in buttermilk. In fact, buttermilk contains less fat than whole milk. It is a cultured dairy product that has a distinctively tart or sour taste. Traditionally it is the liquid by-product of the butter-churning process. Starter cultures from bacterial strains are introduced into skim or low-fat milk, and the milk is held at a controlled temperature for 12 to 14 hours.

While it is best to use real buttermilk when possible, there are some substitutes that can be used in a pinch. Plain yogurt may be substituted for buttermilk (1 cup [230 g] of yogurt = 1 cup [230 g] of buttermilk.) Another trick is to add 1 tablespoon (15 ml) vinegar or lemon juice to 1 cup (235 ml) of milk, and let it stand for 10 minutes before using in the recipe.

a) **Use circle cutter** to cut out rounds.

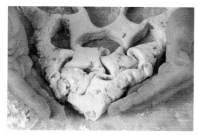

b) **Gently fold** excess dough together to reuse.

c) **Sprinkle** with crumb topping before baking if desired.

Spicing Up CRUMB TOPPING

The basic crumb topping tastes just fine, but ginger lovers will appreciate this extra kick of flavor: simply add a teaspoon of ground ginger or some finely chop up some candied ginger to taste. The warmth of the flavor will permeate all the layers of taste.

Savory Scones

YIELD: **16 wedge scones or 14 round scones (3" [7.6 cm] diameter)**

BAKING TEMPERATURE: **350°F (180°C, gas mark 4) convection mode**

BAKING TIME: **15 to 18 minutes**

Scones don't have to be sweet—they are enjoyed just as much as a savory treat! These buttermilk scones are a perfect way to round out your brunch or as a variation on the dinner roll for the evening meal. Choose from either the combination of smoky flavors of bacon, caramelized onions, and Gruyère cheese or the strong, rustic flavors of blue cheese and pecans. As always, feel free to experiment with other savory ingredients, such as olives and roasted red peppers or a pesto glaze sprinkled with cheese—even a simple pinch of dill alone can totally transform this recipe. Let your imagination and culinary creativity run wild!

Basic Scone Formula

Ingredient	Metric	Weight	Volume
All-purpose* or bread flour	400 g	14.1 oz	3¼ cups
Salt	4 g	0.14 oz	½ tsp
Granulated sugar	56 g	2 oz	¼ cup
Baking powder	24 g	0.84 oz	2 tbsp
Unsweetened butter,	148 g	5.22 oz	10 tbsp
Eggs, whole	82 g	2.90 oz	1 egg + 1 egg white**
Buttermilk	230 g	8.11 oz	1 cup
Egg Wash (page 152)	1 batch	1 batch	1 batch

*When using all-purpose flour, remember to hold back a bit of liquid.

**You can reserve the egg yolk to make an egg wash.

Version 1: Bacon and Caramelized Onion Scones with Grated Gruyère

Ingredient	Metric	Weight	Volume
Caramelized onions	45 g	1.6 oz	⅓ cup
Cooked bacon	45 g	1.6 oz	½ cup (about 5 strips)
Topping: grated Gruyère cheese	40 g	1.41 oz	¼ cup
Ground pepper	1 g	0.03 oz	¼ tsp

Version 2: Blue Cheese Scones with Pecans

Ingredient	Metric	Weight	Volume
Caramelized onions	30 g	1.05 oz	¼ cup
Blue cheese, crumbled	30 g	1.05 oz	¼ cup
Pecans, chopped and toasted	60 g	2.11 oz	⅔ cup

Procedure:

1. Preheat a convection oven to 350°F (180°C, gas mark 4).

2. In a large mixing bowl, sift together the bread flour, salt, granulated sugar, and baking powder (and ground pepper if making the bacon and onion version).

3. Slice the cold butter into small cubes (approximately 1 tablespoon [14 g] each). Using your fingertips, work the butter into the dry ingredients until the butter pieces are no larger than a pea (see Rubbing, page 50).

4. In a separate bowl, whisk together the eggs and buttermilk.

5. Make a depression in the center of the crumbly dry ingredients and pour the liquid ingredients into this well.

6. Using a rubber spatula or a plastic dough scraper, blend the two together by folding the dry ingredients into the wet ingredients.

7. When the batter just comes together and is still a little lumpy, add the savory ingredients and hand mix briefly **(a)**.

8. Place the batter on a flour-dusted surface and fold together using your hands, until the batter is manageable. Do not overwork the batter **(b)**.

9. Shape into a large ball. Press down or roll down until ⅝ inch (1.6 cm) thick. Using a 3-inch (7.6 cm) biscuit or circle cutter, cut out rounds or use a knife to cut wedges. Gently recombine the excess dough (don't pack it together hard, which will toughen it) and roll it out again to continue cutting out shapes. You may have to roll the dough a bit thinner the second time; every time you reroll the dough, it will toughen.

10. Place the scones on a parchment-lined half sheet pan or cookie sheet and let rest for 20 to 30 minutes.

11. Just before baking, brush the tops with an egg wash. Depending on the version of the formula, either sprinkle on some grated Gruyère or decorate with a couple of pecan halves and a sprinkle of blue cheese **(c)**.

12. Bake in the preheated convection oven for 15 to 18 minutes, until golden brown on top. Remove from the oven and let cool on the sheet pan or cookie sheet. (You can place the scones on a wire rack to cool if you need to reuse the sheet pan.)

Blue cheese scones with pecans

a) **Add the savory** ingredients.

c) **Add some grated cheese** or other toppings to the scones.

a) **Fold them into** the dough.

Basic Biscuits

YIELD: **12 round biscuits (3" [7.6 cm] diameter)**

BAKING TEMPERATURE: **350°F (180°C, gas mark 4) convection mode**

BAKING TIME: **15 to 18 minutes**

Breakfast sandwiches are a convenient and easy way to eat breakfast; it's no wonder they are such a hit at the drive-through. But with a little bit of preparation, you can be enjoying your own homemade breakfast sandwich at a fraction of the cost. Biscuits are quick and easy to make and are also easy to freeze and reheat. Before you head out the door, just slice and fill with a fried egg or a slice of ham and cheese, put it into the toaster oven to warm it up, and off you go! Of course, these biscuits go with gravy and aren't just for breakfast, either . . . they make a great addition to dinner (or dessert as the basis for a great strawberry shortcake, too)!

Ingredient	Metric	Weight	Volume
All-purpose* or bread flour	400 g	14.1 oz	3¼ cups
Salt	8 g	0.28 oz	1 tsp
Granulated sugar	20 g	0.7 oz	2 tbsp
Baking powder	24 g	0.84 oz	2 tbsp
Unsweetened butter	140 g	4.93 oz	10 tbsp
Whole milk	230 g	8.11 oz	1 cup
Grated cheddar cheese (optional)	Up to 200 g**	7 oz	1 cup
Caramelized onions, finely chopped (optional)	Up to 200 g**	7 oz	1 cup
Roasted vegetables, finely chopped (optional)	Up to 200 g**	7 oz	1 cup
Egg Wash (page 152)	As needed	As needed	As needed

*When using all-purpose flour, remember to hold back a bit of liquid.

**The total combined weight of all optional ingredients should not exceed 200 g.

Procedure:

1. Preheat a convection oven to 350°F (180°C, gas mark 4).

2. In a large mixing bowl, sift together the flour, salt, granulated sugar, and baking powder.

3. Cut up the *cold* butter into small pieces and add to the dry ingredients. Using your fingers, work the butter in by hand until the butter pieces are no larger than a pea (see Rubbing, page 50).

4. Make a well in the center of the dry ingredients and pour the milk into it.

5. Using a bowl scraper, work the ingredients together. Take the dry ingredients from the outside of the bowl and fold them toward the center into the milk.

6. When the batter is still a bit lumpy, add the cheese or other optional ingredients. The total weight of all optional ingredients combined should not exceed 200 g (7 oz). For example: 200 g of grated cheese, *or* 100 g grated cheese and 100 g caramelized onions, *or* 100 g grated cheese and 50 g caramelized onions and 50 g roasted vegetables **(a)**.

7. Turn out the dough onto a flour-dusted work surface and fold together until you achieve a good working consistency.

8. Using a rolling pin, roll out the dough to approximately 1¼ to 1½ inches (3.2 to 3.8 cm) thick **(b)**. Cut out biscuits using a 3-inch (7.6 cm) circular cookie cutter **(c)**. Gather together the dough scraps to reroll and continue to cut out shapes.

9. Place the dough rounds on a parchment-lined sheet pan and let rest for 20 to 30 minutes, to allow the gluten to relax and retain the shape when baking.

10. Mix up a basic egg wash and brush the tops of the biscuits **(d)**. If desired, you can sprinkle with some grated cheese or top with a few pieces of onion or roasted vegetables.

11. Bake in the preheated convection oven for 15 to 18 minutes, until golden brown on top. Remove from the oven and allow to cool on a wire rack.

a) **Fold in** grated cheese or other ingredients.

b) **Roll out the dough** with a rolling pin.

c) **Cut out** biscuits.

d) **Brush the tops** of the biscuits with egg wash.

Swiss Carrot Cake

YIELD: **1 loaf (9" x 5" x 4" [22.9 x 12.7 x 10.2 cm]) or 12 to 14 medium muffins**

BAKING TEMPERATURE: **325°F (170°C, gas mark 3) convection mode (350°F [180°C, gas mark 4] for muffins)**

BAKING TIME: **50 to 60 minutes (20 to 25 for muffins)**

A delicate hint of nuts sets this carrot cake apart from the familiar version. Hazelnut and almond flour makes its texture slightly denser than traditional American carrot cake and more similar to a banana bread. The carrots add nutrition, contribute to the moistness, and give the cake its warm, orange color. The Swiss Carrot Cake does not have a cream cheese frosting and is topped instead with a simple, lemon-kissed sugar glaze. Just remember to let all cold ingredients warm up to room temperature before mixing together with the melted butter, otherwise the butter will become cold enough to begin to set up again.

Ingredient	Metric	Weight	Volume
Carrots, finely grated	250 g	8.8 oz	2 cups lightly packed (about 4 medium-size carrots)
Eggs, whole	200 g	7 oz	4 eggs
Unsalted butter	200 g	7 oz	14 tbsp
All-purpose or bread flour	350 g	12.3 oz	2¾ cups
Baking powder	18 g	0.63 oz	2 tbsp
Ground cinnamon	2 g	0.07 oz	1 tsp
Salt	3 g	0.1 oz	½ tsp
Lemon zest and juice	1 lemon	1 lemon	1 lemon
Light brown sugar	150 g	5.3 oz	¾ cup
Granulated sugar	150 g	5.3 oz	¾ cup
Almond flour	100 g	3.5 oz	1 cup
Hazelnut flour	100 g	3.5 oz	1¼ cups
Lemon-Sugar Glaze (page 153)	1 batch	1 batch	1 batch

ZESTING a Lemon

The best tool to use when zesting a lemon (or any citrus fruit) is a fine micrograter. It zests only the top layer of the rind containing the essential oils and not the bitter white pith below the surface. This produces light, thin shavings that mix well into any recipe. Run the micrograter over the surface in one direction, turning the lemon as you go. You can also use a lemon zester or vegetable parer; the trimmings must be finely minced with a chef's knife.

Procedure:

1. Preheat a convection oven to 325°F (170°C, gas mark 3). (If making muffins, preheat to 350°F, gas mark 4.)

2. Prepare a 9 x 5 x 4-inch (22.9 x 12.7 x 10.2 cm) loaf pan by spraying the sides and bottom with non-stick baking spray. Cut a piece of parchment paper approximately 16 x 3 inches (40.6 x 7.6 cm) and line the bottom and ends with this single piece.

3. Take the eggs and whole carrots out of the refrigerator and let them come to room temperature (20 to 30 minutes.)

4. While the eggs and carrots are warming up, melt the butter in a small saucepan over low heat. Remove from the heat and allow the butter to cool to lukewarm. (Test the temperature by dipping in your finger; it should feel neutral to the touch.) If the butter cools too much and starts to set up, simply gently reheat it slightly.

5. Sift together the flour, baking powder, ground cinnamon, and salt and set aside.

6. Finely grate the carrots using a box grater and place in a large bowl **(a)**. Zest and juice the lemon. Add the zest and juice to the grated carrots and set aside.

7. Blend together the melted butter, eggs, brown sugar, and granulated sugar until combined. Add the carrots, lemon zest, and lemon juice, and blend. Add the almond and hazelnut flours and mix together. Gently fold the flour mixture into the wet carrot mixture until just combined **(b)**.

8. Fill the loaf pan two-thirds full with batter. If making muffins, fill paper-lined muffin tins two thirds full with batter **(c)**.

9. Bake the cake in the preheated convection oven for 50 to 60 minutes, or until a cake tester comes out clean. If making muffins, bake in the preheated convection oven for 20 to 25 minutes.

10. About 5 to 10 minutes before the cake is done baking, prepare a batch of Lemon-Sugar Glaze.

11. After baking, let the carrot cake sit for 5 minutes before removing from the pan and let it cool on a wire rack.

12. While the carrot cake is still warm, drizzle or brush the glaze onto the top and smooth with a pastry brush if desired **(d)**.

a) **Finely grate the carrots** using a box grater.

b) **Mix the nut flours** and blend.

c) **Portion the batter** into prepared muffin tins or loaf pan.

d) **Apply the lemon-sugar glaze** while the cake or muffins are still warm.

Pumpkin Muffins

YIELD: **15 to 18 muffins or 2 loaves (9" x 4" x 3" [22.9 x 10.2 x 7.6 cm])**

BAKING TEMPERATURE: **350°F (180°C, gas mark 4) convection mode (325°F [170°C, gas mark 3] convection mode for loaves)**

BAKING TIME: **20 to 25 minutes (60 minutes for loaves)**

These muffins are an absolute favorite in our house. Their moist texture, hearty flavor, and spiced warmth make the perfect after-school treat or lunch-box surprise. It calls for pumpkin puree, and canned pure pumpkin is what to look for on the shelves (unless you are making your own—see page 81).

This can be made in a loaf pan, too. To dress up slices into a casual dessert, just warm them in the microwave or with steam on the stovetop (warming in the oven will tend to dry it out) and then top with a dollop of freshly whipped cream sweetened with a bit of sugar and flavored with a pinch of pumpkin pie spice or cinnamon. *Voilà!*

Procedure:

1. Prepare a batch of Crunch Topping or Crumb Topping and refrigerate (can be made up to a week in advance).

2. Prepare muffins tins with nonstick baking spray. Preheat a convection oven to 350°F (180°C, gas mark 4).

3. In a mixing bowl, sift together the flour, cinnamon, nutmeg, cloves, allspice, salt, baking soda, and baking powder, and set aside.

4. In a large mixing bowl, blend together the granulated sugar, vegetable oil, and vanilla extract using a paddle attachment.

Ingredient	Metric	Weight	Volume
All-purpose or bread flour	330 g	11.64 oz	2½ cups
Ground cinnamon	3 g	0.10 oz	1 tsp
Ground nutmeg	1.5 g	0.05 oz	½ tsp
Ground cloves	1.5 g	0.05 oz	½ tsp
Ground allspice	1.5 g	0.05 oz	½ tsp
Salt	4.5 g	0.15 oz	½ tsp
Baking soda	4.4 g	0.15 oz	1 tsp
Baking powder	3 g	0.10 oz	1 tsp
Granulated sugar	500 g	17.63 oz	2½ cups
Vegetable oil	160 g	1.64 oz	¾ cup
Vanilla extract	5 g	0.17 oz	1 tsp
Eggs, whole	150 g	5.29 oz	3 eggs
Pumpkin puree or canned pure pumpkin	340 g	12 oz	1½ cups
Crunch Topping (page 152) *or* Crumb Topping (page 151)	1 batch	1 batch	1 batch

5. Slowly add the eggs one at a time, blending well between each egg, then add the pumpkin puree and mix. Add the dry ingredients mixture and blend, being careful not to overmix. The batter will be rather wet **(a)**.

6. Scoop the batter into the muffin tins, filling two-thirds full, and sprinkle with the Crunch Topping or Crumb Topping. An ice-cream scoop works well for portioning the batter **(b, c)**.

7. Bake in the preheated convection oven for 20 to 25 minutes. Remove from the oven and let stand for 5 minutes before removing from the pans and allowing to cool on a wire rack.

For loaves, prepare two 9 x 4 x 3-inch (22.9 x 10.2 x 7.6 cm) loaf pans with nonstick baking spray. Fill two-thirds full with the batter. Bake at 325°F (170°C, gas mark 3) in a preheated convection oven for 60 minutes.

Fresh PUMPKIN PUREE

Although pumpkin from a can is convenient, making your own puree has definite benefits: It's fresher and nothing can compare to its complex, roasted sweet flavor. Another benefit—you have all those seeds to roast and eat, too!

Heat the oven to 400°F (200°C, gas mark 6). Slice a sugar pumpkin in half, remove the seeds, and place the two halves cut side up in a baking dish. Roast for about an hour or until very soft inside, then remove from the oven and let cool. Scrape out all the pumpkin's flesh, leaving only an empty shell or rind behind. Place the scraped pumpkin in a food processor and puree until smooth. Store immediately in the refrigerator for up to two days, or in the freezer for up to two months. Drain any excess moisture that separates before using.

a) **Add the dry ingredients** to the wet mixture and blend.

b) **Scoop the batter** into the baking forms.

c) **Sprinkle** with topping.

Southwest Corn Bread

YIELD:	**One 9" (22.9 cm) pan for corn bread *or* 12 small muffins**
BAKING TEMPERATURE:	**360°F (182°C, gas mark 4) convection mode**
BAKING TIME:	**20 to 25 minutes**

As a boy growing up in Switzerland, I spent my days counting down the hours until I could watch my favorite western television show, *Winnetou*. I didn't learn until years later that it was actually filmed in Turkey, but it really didn't matter; the landscape and drama had captivated my imagination of the Wild West forever.

Corn bread is evocative of the American West. I can just imagine a group of cowboys, exhausted from their hours of driving cattle, finally sitting down together for the evening meal at the campfire, baking up a skillet of corn bread from the simplest of ingredients. This version has the same rustic appeal, with some added flavor and texture. Bake it in a pan and cut into wedges, or make as muffins to enjoy anytime. I baked them in fluted tart pans for a decorative effect.

Ingredient	Metric	Weight	Volume
Bacon, uncooked (optional)	150 g	5.29 oz	15 strips
All-purpose or bread flour	156 g	5.5 oz	1¼ tsp
Baking powder	7 g	0.24 oz	2 tsp
Granulated sugar	25 g	0.88 oz	¼ cup
Salt	3 g	0.1 oz	¼ tsp
Cornmeal	136 g	4.79 oz	¾ cup
Eggs, whole	100 g	3.52 oz	2 eggs
Vegetable oil	54 g	1.9 oz	¼ cup
Whole milk	128 g	4.51 oz	½ cup
Maple syrup or honey	50 g	1.76 oz	3 tbsp
Corn niblets	215 g	7.58 oz	½ cup
Sharp cheddar cheese, grated	75 g	2.64 oz	1 cup

Procedure:

1. Preheat a convection oven to 360°F (182°C, or gas mark 4). Prepare baking forms (cake pan or muffin tins) with nonstick baking spray.

2. Sauté the bacon, if using, in a heavy skillet until cooked, remove from the pan, and let rest on several paper towels to absorb excess fat. Dice into small pieces.

3. Sift together the flour, baking powder, granulated sugar, salt, and cornmeal into a mixing bowl and set aside.

4. In a large mixing bowl, whisk together the eggs, vegetable oil, milk, and maple syrup or honey.

5. Stir the dry ingredients into the egg mixture until a smooth consistency is achieved.

6. Carefully fold in the corn, grated cheese, and optional cooked bacon **(a)**.

7. Pour the batter into the prepared baking forms and garnish with some additional cheese, corn, or fire-roasted peppers **(b, c)**.

8. Bake in the preheated convection oven for 20 to 25 minutes, until golden brown on top.

9. Remove from the pan and allow to cool on a wire rack.

a) **Add the corn** to the batter and blend.

b) **Portion** into baking forms.

b) **Garnish** with desired toppings.

Zucchini Bread

YIELD: **1 loaf (9" x 4" x 3" [22.9 x 10.2 x 7.6 cm]) or 10 to 12 muffins**

BAKING TEMPERATURE: **325°F (170°C, gas mark 3) convection mode (350°F [180°C, gas mark 4] convection mode for muffins)**

BAKING TIME: **60 minutes (20 to 25 minutes for muffins)**

The plight of the vegetable gardener is what to do with all those prolific zucchini plants that produce one squash after the other, seemingly overnight. If you have ever planted zucchini, then you know what I mean!

With its raisins and walnuts, this recipe makes the perfect snack to have on hand for any time of day. It's so moist and delicious—children won't even mind the added nutrition! For extra health, use half bread flour and half whole wheat flour. You will barely notice the change in texture.

Ingredient	Metric	Weight	Volume
Zucchini, finely grated (do not peel)	175 g	6.17 oz	1 cup loosely packed
All-purpose or bread flour	260 g	9.17 oz	2 cups
Ground cinnamon	1 g	0.03 oz	½ tsp
Salt	8 g	0.28 oz	1 tsp
Baking soda	4 g	0.14 oz	1 tsp
Baking powder	1.5 g	0.05 oz	½ tsp
Granulated sugar	120 g	4.23 oz	½ cup
Light brown sugar, packed	110 g	3.88 oz	½ cup
Vanilla extract	5 g	0.17 oz	1 tsp
Eggs, whole	100 g	3.52 oz	2 eggs
Vegetable oil	130 g	4.58 oz	⅔ cup
Raisins	55 g	1.94 oz	½ cup
Walnuts, chopped	50 g	1.76 oz	½ cup
Rolled oats	As needed	As needed	As needed
Lemon-Sugar Glaze (page 153, optional)	1 batch	1 batch	1 batch

Procedure:

1. Preheat a convection oven to 325°F (170°C, gas mark 3) and grease a 9 x 4 x 3-inch (22.9 x 10.2 x 7.6 cm) loaf pan.

2. Sift together the flour, cinnamon, salt, baking soda, and baking powder into a bowl and set aside.

3. In a large mixing bowl, blend together the granulated sugar, light brown sugar, vanilla extract, eggs, and vegetable oil.

4. Gently add the dry ingredients to the wet and fold in.

5. Stir in the grated zucchini, raisins, and walnuts (**a**).

6. Fill the prepared loaf pans two thirds full with batter and sprinkle the top with rolled oats (**b, c**).

7. Bake in the preheated convection oven for 60 minutes.

8. Allow the pan to stand for 10 to 15 minutes before removing the bread. Remove the bread and let cool completely on a wire rack.

9. If you would like a glaze on top, apply Lemon-Sugar Glaze while the zucchini bread is still warm (d).

For muffins: Prepare the batter and fill muffin tins two-thirds full. Bake at 350°F (180°C, gas mark 4) in a preheated convection oven for 20 to 25 minutes.

a) **Use a hand grater** or food processor to finely grate the zucchini.

b) **Pour the batter** into the pans.

b) **Sprinkle the top** with rolled oats.

d) **Drizzle or brush on** Lemon-Sugar Glaze if desired.

Banana Muffins

YIELD: **12 to 14 small muffins or 1 loaf (9" x 4" x 3" [22.9 x 10.2 x 7.6 cm]) plus a few muffins**

BAKING TEMPERATURE: **350°F (180°C, gas mark 4) convection mode (325°F [170°C, gas mark 3] convection mode for loaves)**

BAKING TIME: **20 to 25 minutes (60 minutes for loaf)**

Not everyone has a zucchini jungle taking over the garden, but we have all had a couple of bananas that have been ignored on the countertop and have crossed over to "the dark side." Thankfully, these are the best kind for making banana muffins!

The origin of banana muffins is unknown, although it started to appear in cookbooks during the 1930s, about the same time that baking powder became widely available to the home baker. Bananas are great sources of nutrients, especially potassium, and this muffin's mild flavor appeals to all palates.

Procedure:

1. Bring the butter and eggs to room temperature. Prepare baking forms (muffin tins or loaf pans) with nonstick baking spray.

2. Preheat a convection oven to 350°F (180°C, gas mark 4).

3. Sift together the flour, baking powder, cinnamon, and salt into a mixing bowl and set aside.

4. Prepare the Crunch Topping.

5. Either by hand or in a stand mixer using a paddle attachment, mash the bananas, then slowly add the room-temperature eggs and vanilla extract. Set aside.

Ingredient	Metric	Weight	Volume
Unsalted butter	113 g	4 oz	½ cup
Eggs, whole	150 g	5.29 oz	3 eggs
All-purpose or bread flour	265 g	9.34 oz	2 cups
Baking powder	14 g	0.49 oz	3¼ tsp
Ground cinnamon	0.5 g	0.02 oz	¼ tsp
Salt	2 g	0.07 oz	¼ tsp
Crunch Topping (page 152)	1 batch	1 batch	1 batch
Bananas, overripe	375 g	13.22 oz	1½ cups mashed (3-4 bananas)
Granulated sugar	155 g	5.46 oz	¾ cup
Vanilla extract	5 g	0.17 oz	3½ tsp
Chocolate chips	125 g	4.4 oz	1 scant cup
Walnuts, chopped	75 g	2.64 oz	¾ cup

6. In a stand mixer, cream the butter until light in color and texture. Add the granulated sugar and continue to cream (**a**).

7. Slowly add the eggs and banana mixture to the creamed sugar and butter and continue to cream the mixture until eggs are incorporated.

8. Fold the flour mixture into the wet ingredients and mix by hand.

9. Add the chocolate chips and chopped walnuts and mix just until evenly incorporated (**b**).

10. Fill the muffin tins two-thirds full with the batter and sprinkle with the Crunch Topping (**c**).

11. Bake in the preheated convection oven for 20 to 25 minutes, or until a toothpick test comes out clean.

12. Let the muffins stand for 5 minutes before removing from the baking tins and placing on a wire rack to fully cool. Muffins baked in paper forms can be placed directly in the forms on a wire rack.

Loaves: Fill the prepared loaf pans two-thirds full with batter. Bake in a preheated convection oven at 325°F (170°C, gas mark 3) for 60 minutes.

a) **Cream the butter and sugar** together until light in color and texture.

b). **Fold in the nuts** and chocolate into the batter.

c) **Portion the batter** into the baking cups.

Tirolean Chocolate Muffins

YIELD:	**10 to 12 medium-size muffins or 1 loaf (9" x 4" x 3" [22.9 x 10.2 x 7.6 cm])**
BAKING TEMPERATURE:	**350°F (180°C, gas mark 4) convection mode (325°F [170°C, gas mark 3] convection mode for loaf)**
BAKING TIME:	**20 to 25 minutes (60 to 70 minutes for loaf)**

Hazelnut and bittersweet chocolate—be forewarned, this combination can be habit forming! Thank goodness, you can make one loaf and freeze the other for when the craving hits you later on.

Hazelnuts, either ground into a flour or chopped into chunks, have a distinct nutty flavor that complements many other flavors, including chocolate and orange. Widely used for baking in Europe, hazelnuts are beginning to grow in popularity in North America. Although this cake does not appear to have a specific origin, I enjoyed something very similar one afternoon sitting in a tiny café in the foothills of the Tirolean Alps. The flavors of chocolate and nuts, paired with good strong coffee . . . it was bliss.

Ingredient	Metric	Weight	Volume
Unsalted butter	126 g	4.44 oz	9 tbsp
Eggs, whole	200 g	7.05 oz	4 eggs
All-purpose flour	120 g	4.23 oz	1 cup
Baking powder	9 g	0.31 oz	2 ½ tsp
Granulated sugar	200 g	7.05 oz	1 cup
Salt	2 g	0.07 oz	¼ tsp
Hazelnut flour	200 g	7.05 oz	2 ¾ cups
Bittersweet chocolate chunks	150 g	5.29 oz	1 cup
Crumb Topping (page 151, optional)	1 batch	1 batch	1 batch
Powdered sugar (optional)	As needed	As needed	As needed

Procedure:

1. Bring the butter and eggs to room temperature.

2. Preheat a convection oven to 350°F (180°C, gas mark 4) and prepare muffin tins with nonstick baking spray and parchment paper.

3. Sift together the flour and baking powder in a bowl and set aside.

4. Optional: Prepare the Crumb Topping and set aside.

5. In a stand mixer using a paddle attachment, cream together the butter, granulated sugar, and salt.

6. Slowly add the eggs to the butter mixture one at a time, mixing well until light and creamy in color.

7. Fold in the hazelnut flour by hand until just incorporated.

8. Add half of the all-purpose flour mixture and fold in by hand.

9. Add the remainder of the flour along with the bittersweet chocolate chunks and gently fold in until just combined **(a)**.

10. Fill prepared muffin tins two-thirds full with batter **(b)**. Sprinkle Crumb Topping on top if desired **(c)**.

11. Bake in the convection oven for 20 to 25 minutes, or until a cake tester comes out clean from the middle.

12. Remove from the oven and let stand for 5 minutes before removing from pan. Let cool completely on a wire rack. When cool, dust with powdered sugar if desired.

Loaves: Pour the batter two-thirds full into the prepared loaf pan. Bake in a convection oven at 325°F (170°C, gas mark 3) for 60 to 70 minutes.

a) **Toss the chocolate** chunks with the remainder of flour before mixing in.

b) **Fill** the muffin cups.

c) **Top with crumb topping** if desired.

Bran Muffins

YIELD: **18 to 20 muffins or 2 loaves (9" x 4" x 3" [22.9 x 10.2 x 7.6 cm])**

BAKING TEMPERATURE: **350°F (180°C, gas mark 4) convection mode (325°F [170°C, gas mark 3] convection mode for loaves)**

BAKING TIME: **20 to 25 minutes (50 to 60 minutes for loaves)**

If you know someone who is not a big bran fan, put this muffin to the taste test! Its moist texture and plump raisins are a welcome change from the dry, crumbly bran muffins of the past. Bran is the outermost layer of the wheat kernel that is left over from the milling process of refined flours. Adding it to baked goods boosts the fiber level in your diet. You can usually find unprocessed wheat bran in the cereal aisle at your local grocery store. The thin, small flakes resemble very fine sawdust and are not to be confused with bran flakes, a bran-based cereal that looks like cornflakes.

Ingredient	Metric	Weight	Volume
Eggs, whole	125 g	4.4 oz	2 eggs + 1 yolk
Unsalted butter	125 g	4.4 oz	9 tbsp
Bread flour	450 g	15.87 oz	3½ cups
Ground cinnamon	1 g	0.03 oz	½ tsp
Baking soda	14 g	0.49 oz	2¾ tsp
Baking powder	10 g	0.35 oz	2¾ tsp
Salt	7 g	0.24 oz	1 tsp
Light brown sugar	210 g	7.4 oz	2¼ cups (packed)
Vanilla extract	5 g	0.17 oz	1 tsp
Molasses	225 g	7.93 oz	½ cup
Unsweetened applesauce	107 g	3.7 oz	½ cup
Unprocessed wheat bran	210 g	7.4 oz	2 cups
Whole milk	670 g	23.63 oz	2⅔ cups
Golden raisins	140 g	4.93 oz	1 cup
Dark raisins	140 g	4.93 oz	1 cup

Procedure:

1. Bring the eggs and butter to room temperature. Preheat a convection oven to 350°F (180°C, gas mark 4). Prepare muffin cups with nonstick baking spray or liners.

2. In a mixing bowl, sift together the bread flour, ground cinnamon, baking soda, baking powder, and salt.

3. In a mixing bowl or stand mixer, combine the butter, light brown sugar, and vanilla extract, and cream together until light in color and texture.

4. Slowly add the eggs, molasses, and unsweetened applesauce, mixing well until thoroughly incorporated.

5. Add the wheat bran and mix until combined.

6. Alternate adding the milk and flour mixture to the creamed butter and egg mixture. Blend well between additions. The resultant mixture should have a smooth consistency (a).

7. Stir the golden and dark raisins into the batter (b).

8. Fill the prepared muffin cups two-thirds full with the batter. For a decorative effect, sprinkle a bit of bran on top of the muffins before baking (c).

9. Bake in the preheated convection oven for 20 to 25 minutes or until a cake tester inserted into the middle comes out clean.

10. Remove from the oven and allow to cool on a wire rack.

NOT Craving Raisins?

Although raisins are sweet sources of antioxidants and a good source of iron and potassium, it doesn't mean that everyone adores them. If raisins just aren't your cup of tea, feel free to substitute other dried fruit such as cranberries, cherries, apricots, or prunes. You will still have the additional benefits of flavor, texture, and fiber, no matter which type of dried fruit you use. Just cut up into raisin-size chunks before adding to the batter.

a) **Alternate** adding the milk and flour mixtures.

b) **Stir** the raisins into the batter.

c) **Sprinkle some extra bran** over the tops of the muffins for a decorative effect.

English Muffins

YIELD:	**12 (3½" [9 cm] diameter)**
BAKING TEMPERATURE:	**360°F (182°C, gas mark 4) convection mode**
BAKING TIME:	**25 minutes**

Technically this formula is not a "quick bread;" the dough uses a unique combination of both baking powder and yeast and falls into its own category. Typically English muffins are made in rings on a stovetop griddle. With this version, however, you can use the English muffin rings to bake them right in the oven. Whole wheat flour and the seven-grain seed mix give these English muffins a wholesome, nutty texture.

Despite its name, it is said the English muffin was first made in the United States by Samuel B. Thomas from his mother's tea cake recipe. Serve them toasted along with butter and jam, or use them as the basis of heartier fare, including breakfast sandwiches and the decadent Eggs Benedict.

Poolish

Ingredient	Metric	Weight	Volume
All-purpose or bread flour	170 g	6 oz	1⅓ cups
Water	170 g	6 oz	¾ cup + 1 tbsp
Instant yeast	0.25 g	Pinch	Pinch

Soaker (optional)

Ingredient	Metric	Weight	Volume
7-grain mixture*	50 g	1.76 oz	⅓ cup
Water	50 g	1.76 oz	⅓ cup

* Seven-grain or five-grain mixtures of assorted grains and seeds, such as cracked whole wheat berries, rye, oats, brown rice, flaxseed, barley, triticale, oat bran, or corn, are available from specialty stores, mail order, or Internet sources.

Final Dough

Ingredient	Metric	Weight	Volume
Whole milk	170 g	6 oz	⅔ cup
All-purpose or bread flour	150 g	5.29 oz	1¼ cups
Whole wheat flour	50 g	1.75 oz	⅓ cup
Honey	20 g	0.70 oz	1 tbsp
Cornstarch	14 g	0.49 oz	2 tbsp
Instant yeast	3 g	0.10 oz	½ tsp
Salt	5 g	0.17 oz	½ tsp
Baking powder	8 g	0.28 oz	2 tsp
Unsalted butter, melted	28 g	1 oz	2 tbsp
Cornmeal, coarse ground	As needed	As needed	As needed

Procedure:

Day before baking:

1. Prepare the poolish: In a mixing bowl, combine the flour, water, and instant yeast. Cover with plastic wrap and let rest overnight at room temperature.

2. In a separate container, soak the 7-grain mixture in the water and let stand overnight at room temperature.

Baking day:

3. Preheat a convection oven to 360°F (182°C, gas mark 4).

4. Line a sheet pan with parchment paper. Spray the insides of the English muffin rings with nonstick baking spray or grease them with butter. Place the rings on the parchment-lined sheet pan and sprinkle some coarse cornmeal into the center of the rings **(a)**.

5. Set aside some cornmeal for topping.

6. In a microwave or saucepan, warm the milk to 80°F (27°C).

7. Pour the warm milk into the bowl of a 5-quart (5 L) stand mixer. Add the flour, whole wheat flour, honey, cornstarch, instant yeast, salt, baking powder, melted butter, poolish, and soaked grains—do not drain the soaker **(b)**.

8. Using a dough hook, mix the ingredients together at a low speed for about 6 minutes.

9. Cover the bowl with plastic wrap and allow to rest at room temperature for 1½ hours **(c)**.

10. Use a medium-size ice-cream scoop dipped in water to portion out the dough into the rings. The dough should fill about one-third of each ring.

11. Using wet fingers, press the dough out evenly within each ring and sprinkle the tops with some cornmeal **(d)**.

12. Cover the tops of the rings with a sheet of parchment paper and place another sheet pan on top **(e)**.

13. Allow to proof at room temperature for 1 hour, or until the dough has reached the top of the ring.

14. Bake in the preheated convection oven for 25 minutes, removing the top sheet pan for the last 5 minutes of the baking process.

15. Allow the muffins to cool for about 5 minutes before removing from the rings. Cool completely on a wire rack before serving. Split the muffins in half using a fork, or cut in half with a knife.

a) **The ring**s are on a parchment-lined sheet pan with some sprinkled cornmeal.

b) **Add the soaked grains** and mix the ingredients together on low speed.

c) **Pour the dough** into a proofing container, cover, and allow to rest.

d) **Use wet fingers** to press the dough evenly into the rings.

e) **Cover the tops** with parchment paper and another sheet pan.

Mixed-Berry Muffins

YIELD:	**15 muffins**
BAKING TEMPERATURE:	**360°F (182°C, gas mark 4) convection mode)**
BAKING TIME:	**20 to 25 minutes**

With this recipe, enjoy a taste of summer any time of year. If you stock up on berries (the best are fresh-picked and in season), you can freeze them for later use. Frozen berries are resistant to damage and remain whole during the mixing process, but fresh berries will taste great, too.

Procedure:

1. Bring the butter to room temperature. Preheat a convection oven to 360°F (182°C, gas mark 4).

2. Prepare muffins tins (or other small individual baking forms) with nonstick baking spray or line with paper muffin cups. Combine eggs, sour cream, and lemon zest in a bowl and let warm to about 60° to 65°F (16° to 18°C).

3. Prepare the Crumb Topping and refrigerate.

4. Sift together the flour, salt, baking soda, and baking powder into a mixing bowl. Stir in cornmeal. Remove ¼ cup (33 g) of this mixture, and toss it with the frozen berries to coat **(a)**. Place the flour-coated berries back in the freezer until ready to use.

5. Either by hand or in a stand mixer using a paddle attachment, cream together the butter and granulated sugar until light in color and texture.

Ingredient	Metric	Weight	Volume
All-purpose or bread flour	313 g	11 oz	2½ cups
Corn meal	50 g	1.7 oz	⅓ cup
Unsalted butter	200 g	7 oz	14 tbsp
Granulated sugar	230 g	8.1 oz	1 cup
Eggs, whole	100 g	3.5 oz	2 eggs
Lemon zest	2 lemons	2 lemons	2 lemons
Sour cream	200 g	8 oz	8 oz
Baking powder	7 g	0.24 oz	2 tbsp
Baking soda	4 g	0.14 oz	1 tsp
Salt	4 g	0.14 oz	½ tsp
Frozen blueberries	100 g	3.5 oz	¾ cup
Frozen raspberries	100 g	3.5 oz	¾ cup
Crumb Topping (page 151)	1 batch	1 batch	1 batch

6. Alternate adding the dry and wet ingredients to the creamed butter and sugar mixture. Fold in by hand to prevent overmixing and gluten development. Be sure to scrape the sides of the bowl between additions **(b)**.

7. Add the flour-coated frozen berries to the remaining flour mixture, and gently fold into the batter. (The frozen berries will cause the butter in the recipe to chill down, and at this point, the batter will thicken.)

8. Scoop the batter into the muffin tins, filling two thirds full, and sprinkle with the Crumb Topping **(c)**.

9. Bake in the convection oven for 20 to 25 minutes, or until an inserted cake tester comes out clean. Allow to cool on a wire rack.

a) **Gently coat the frozen berries** with the reserved flour mixture.

b) **Mixing** is best done by hand to prevent gluten development.

c) **Just before baking,** sprinkle the tops with Crumb Topping.

Whole Wheat Cinnamon Raisin Bagels

YIELD:	**9 to 10 bagels**
BAKING TEMPERATURE:	**380°F (190°C, gas mark 5) convection mode)**
BAKING TIME:	**18 to 20 minutes**

This formula does not fit neatly into any of the three categories (quick breads, enriched doughs, or laminated doughs), but it is still perfect for this book. The most difficult part about making a bagel at home is the mixing. The dough is very stiff, and it is hard work for most home mixers. Take your time, and have a spray bottle filled with water on hand to help lubricate the dough during the mixing process.

Ingredient	Metric	Weight	Volume
Bread flour	250 g	8.8 oz	2 cups
High-gluten flour*	250 g	8.8 oz	2 cups
Whole wheat flour	125 g	4.4 oz	1 cup
Water, 72°F (22°C)	370 g	13 oz	1½ cups
Yeast, instant	4 g	0.14 oz	1 tsp.
Salt	12 g	0.42 oz	1½ tsp.
Milk, diastatic*	10 g	0.35 oz	3¼ tsp.
Dark raisins, (optional)	125 g	4.4 oz	1 cup
Cinnamon Sugar (optional, page 151)	1 batch	1 batch	1 batch

* Available from specialty stores, mail order, or Internet sources.

Water mixture

Ingredient	Metric	Weight	Volume
Water	2 liters	4 lb 6 oz	8 cups
Honey or corn syrup	180 g	6.3 oz	⅔ cup

Procedure:

Day before baking:

1. Place the flours, water, instant yeast, salt, and malt into the bowl of a 5-quart (5 L) stand mixer with a dough hook attachment. Mix on low speed for approximately 4 minutes, then increase the speed to medium and continue to mix for another 2 to 4 minutes. If desired, add the raisins and 25 grams (2 ½ tbsp) of the Cinnamon Sugar mixture to the dough at the end of this mixing period, reserving the rest for dipping the bagels).

Note: This is a stiff dough. If the machine is straining, a couple of squirts of water from a spray bottle should help. Turn the mixer off and let it rest if the mixing is too strenuous.

2. After mixing, divide the dough into 110 gram (3.8 oz.) units. Take each unit and, using your hands on a floured surface, roll into a log approximately ¾ inch (2 cm) thick and 10 inches (25 cm) long. Make the ends a bit thicker than the center.

3. Make a ring around your hand with the log, and pinch the ends together with some pinching pressure. Place the dough seam onto the work surface, and roll the dough with a downward pressure to compress the ends together. Try to make the bagel ring as uniform as possible (**a, b**).

4. Place the bagels on a parchment-lined sheet pan sprayed with nonstick cooking spray and cover them with a tent of plastic wrap. (Hint: Large, clear, unscented garbage bags work well for this.) Place in the refrigerator overnight (c).

Baking day:

1. Preheat a convection oven to 380°F (190°C, gas mark 5). Combine the water and honey (or corn syrup) in a large pot and bring to a boil. Use a mesh strainer to skim off any impurities from the honey that rise to the top (d).

2. Remove the bagels from the refrigerator, and place them, 2 or 3 at a time, into the boiling water for 10 to 15 seconds. (The bagels should not be crowded or touching.) Carefully turn them over with a slotted spoon and boil for another 10 to 15 seconds. The bagels should float; if they do not, let the remaining bagels rest at room temperature for about 30 minutes (e).

3. Place each batch of boiled bagels onto a cooling rack to drip dry. If desired, dip the bagels into the remaining Cinnamon Sugar mix—be sure that the bagel is almost dry to the touch, or else the sugar will dissolve. Feel free to use other toppings as well, such as sesame, poppy, or sunflower seeds (f).

4. Place the prepared bagels on a parchment-lined sheet pan, and bake in the preheated convection oven for 18 to 20 minutes, or until a golden brown color is achieved. Remove from the oven, and transfer the bagels to a cooling rack. Cool for at least 30 minutes before eating. To keep the bagels soft, store them in an airtight container for a day or two. Bagels can be placed in plastic bags and frozen for up to a month.

a) **Seal the ends** of the bagel together.

b) **Roll the ring** with downward pressure to compress the ends together.

c) **Place the bagels** on the prepared sheet pan and cover with plastic before refrigerating overnight.

d) **Use a mesh strainer** to remove any impurities from the boiling water.

e) **Carefully boil the bagels** for 10 to 15 seconds on each side, turning them with a slotted spoon.

f) **Dip the boiled bagels** into Cinnamon Sugar or other topping before baking.

CHAPTER FIVE

Enriched Dough

ONE DEFINITION OF *ENRICH* IS TO MAKE RICHER, and enriched doughs with their pure butter, eggs, or sugar certainly live up to that etymology. These doughs are just as enriching as they are enriched. What I mean is, this particular set of formulas brings an array of characteristics and sensory experiences to the table, literally and figuratively.

I love all types of bread, from a classic baguette to a tangy sourdough, and everything in between. But enriched doughs hold a special place in my heart. I have many great memories of recalling stories over a morning buttered brioche or celebrating a quiet evening moment with a Christmas stollen. That's not to say that I don't have great memories shared over a sourdough and cold cuts, but the mood and atmosphere are decidedly different.

Making any yeasted bread is a labor of love compared with the almost instant gratification you get with quick breads, but I hope you have the intention of exploring at least a few of the formulas in this section. While certain aspects of making enriched doughs may prove to be somewhat challenging, there are also some more forgiving aspects. For instance, it is nearly impossible to overdevelop an enriched dough (unlike, say, a classic baguette dough). The trickiest part of mixing an enriched dough is incorporating the fat, but once you have achieved that, the rest is easy. Most enriched doughs are baked in a baking form, so there is not a lot of tricky shaping, either.

In short, the results are well worth the time and effort. Once you understand the basic principles of working with yeasted doughs and you log some baking hours, you will become more fluent in your "dialogue" with the dough. Your sensory perception will be heightened. You'll see that it's a good time to incorporate the butter, you'll hear when it's time to stop, and you'll *feel* when the dough is ready to bake. It takes time, but each time you bake, you'll experience new things about bread and dough that may just surprise you. And isn't life better with surprises?

Classic Brioche

YIELD: **2 loaves (9" x 5" x 4" [22.9 x 12.7 x 10.2 cm])**

BAKING TEMPERATURE: **330°F (165°C, gas mark 3) convection mode**

BAKING TIME: **30 to 35 minutes**

Dating back to at least the 1400s, brioche is French in origin and is a sweet, rich bread with a tender crumb structure and a golden, flaky crust. Its tender and delicate properties make it feel more like a pastry than a bread. In fact, urban legend has it that Marie Antoinette was referring to the brioche when she was quoted as saying, "If they have no bread, let them eat cake," translated from, *"S'ils n'ont plus de pain, qu'ils mangent de la brioche."* While the original source of this quote is not settled among historians, the fact that the enriched, buttery brioche has cakelike qualities is not disputed among bakers.

Ingredient	Metric	Weight	Volume	Baker's %
All-purpose*or bread flour	530 g	18.6 oz	4¼ cups	100
Granulated sugar	50 g	1.76 oz	¼ cup	9.4
Instant yeast, preferably osmotolerant	14 g	0.49 oz	4 tsp	2.6
Salt	8 g	0.28 oz	1½ tsp	1.5
Lemon zest	⅓ lemon	⅓ lemon	⅓ lemon	n/a
Whole milk	200 g	7 oz	¾ cup	37.7
Unsalted butter	200 g	7 oz	14 tbsp	37.7
Eggs, whole	50 g	1.76 oz	1 egg	9.4
Egg yolks	50 g	1.76 oz	2 yolks	9.4
Egg Wash (page 152)	As needed	As needed	As needed	n/a
Pearl sugar for topping (optional)	As needed	As needed	As needed	n/a
Cinnamon Sugar for topping (page 151, optional)	As needed	As needed	As needed	n/a

*If using all-purpose flour, hold back a bit when initially adding the milk, but do not hesitate to add more liquid so that the dough will come together.

Procedure:

Day before baking:

1. Before beginning, make certain that your liquid ingredients (milk, eggs, egg yolks) and butter are cold.

2. In the bowl of a 5-quart (5 L) stand mixer, mix the flour, granulated sugar, instant yeast, salt, milk, eggs, egg yolks, and lemon zest at low speed until cleanup stage.

3. While the ingredients are mixing, make the butter pliable by hammering it with a rolling pin. (See Mixing an Enriched Dough, page 60.)

4. Increase the mixing speed to medium and slowly start to add the butter to the dough in stages. Remember to wait between additions until the sticky, slapping noise in the mixer has subsided.

5. Mix until all the butter has been incorporated into the dough and the dough is well developed with a nice gluten structure. Check the dough with a gluten window test (see page 57)—you should be able to stretch a nice thin membrane without tearing (a).

6. Remove the dough from the mixer and work into a ball. Gently press it down to flatten and wrap tightly in plastic wrap. Place the dough in the freezer for a minimum of 6 hours. The dough can remain frozen for up to 2 weeks (b).

7. The night before baking, take the dough out of the freezer and transfer into the refrigerator for 12 hours.

Baking day:

1. Remove the dough from the refrigerator and allow it to warm up at room temperature for about 20 minutes.

2. Using a scale and bench scraper, divide the dough into 50 g increments.

3. Work the units into small balls.

4. Spray 2 loaf pans with nonstick cooking spray and place 10 units of dough into each loaf pan 2 rows of 5 dough balls (c).

5. Cover with plastic wrap and let the dough proof until the dough doubles in size (about 1 to 2 hours, depending on the room temperature and the temperature of the dough when taken out of the refrigerator).

6. Mix up the egg wash and preheat a convection oven to 330°F (165°C, gas mark 3).

7. When the dough has doubled in size, brush the tops of the loaves with the egg wash. For a decorative touch, add some pearl sugar or cinnamon sugar to the tops (d). Bake in the preheated convection oven for 30 to 35 minutes, or until the tops have a nice rich brown color.

a) **Mix the dough** until it is fully developed.

b) **Wrap the flattened dough** in plastic and freeze.

c) **Place the dough** units in the prepared loaf pan.

d) **Sprinkle some pearl sugar** or cinnamon sugar on the tops if desired.

Lemon Brioche Doughnuts

YIELD:	**15 doughnuts *or* 1 brioche loaf and 8 doughnuts**
BAKING TEMPERATURE:	**340°F (171°C, gas mark 4) convection mode**
BAKING TIME:	**20 minutes**

The bright citrus tones of lemon are throughout this baked brioche version of a doughnut. This formula starts with the Classic Brioche dough formula, which can be mixed and frozen for up to 2 weeks before baking. Lemon Curd can be made up to 3 days in advance. Lemon-Almond Glaze can be made a day ahead, and Lemon Cream is easily whipped up on baking day. If you plan ahead, the making of this doughnut is not as complicated as it may first appear. Serve it at formal weekend brunch or even as a dessert—it's that spectacular!

Ingredient	Metric	Weight	Volume
Classic Brioche (page 100)	1 batch	1 batch	1 batch
Lemon Curd (page 153)	1 batch	1 batch	1 batch
Lemon-Almond Glaze (page 152)	1 batch	1 batch	1 batch
Lemon Cream (page 152)	1 batch	1 batch	1 batch
Pearl sugar for topping	As needed	As needed	As needed
Powdered sugar for topping	As needed	As needed	As needed

Procedure:

Day before baking:

1. Mix one batch of Classic Brioche dough.

2. Mix one batch of Lemon Curd (can be made up to 3 days in advance).

Baking day:

1. Mix one batch of Lemon-Almond Glaze (can be made up to 2 days in advance).

2. Remove the brioche dough from the refrigerator and let it warm up at room temperature for 20 minutes.

3. Spray 15 fluted tartlet pans (3-inch [7.6 cm] diameter) with nonstick cooking spray and place on a sheet pan. This process can also be done without using the tartlet pans.

4. Using a scale and bench scraper, divide the dough into 70 g units.

5. Using a rolling pin, flatten out each unit to about ¼-inch (6 mm) thick.

6. Take the prepared and chilled Lemon Curd and place about 1 tablespoon (14 g) of curd in the center of each piece of dough.

7. Bring the four corners of the dough toward the center over the curd and pinch them together. Pinch together the seams to seal in the curd **(a)**.

8. Turn the pouch over so that the seam sides are down and gently shape into rounds. Place, seam side down, in fluted tartlet pans sprayed with non-stick baking spray **(b)**.

9. Cover with plastic wrap and let proof until the dough doubles in size (between 1 and 2 hours).

10. Preheat a convection oven to 340°F (171°C, gas mark 4).

11. After proofing, fill the Lemon-Almond Glaze into a pastry bag and pipe or spoon about 1 table-spoon (14 g) onto the tops of each filled brioche **(c)**.

12. Sprinkle the top of the glaze with some pearl sugar and dust heavily with some powdered sugar **(d)**.

13. Bake in the preheated convection oven for about 20 minutes.

14. Remove from the oven and allow to cool in the tartlet pans on a wire rack.

15. In the meantime, prepare a batch of the Lemon Cream.

16. When the brioches are completely cooled, slice them in half with a serrated knife. Spread some of the Lemon Cream on the bottom and replace the tops. Serve and enjoy immediately (see note below).

Note: Because these Lemon Brioche Doughnuts are made with components that contain eggs and dairy, they should be refrigerated if not consumed immediately and for no longer than 24 hours. The quality, texture, and flavor are best when fresh.

a) **Fill the dough pieces** with the lemon curd and pinch the seams to seal.

b) **Gently shape the dough** into rounds and place in a prepared baking form.

c) **Pipe the Lemon-Almond Glaze** onto the tops.

d) **The tops are sprinkled** with pearl sugar and dusted with powdered sugar.

Pumpkin Cream Brioche

YIELD:	**15 brioches**
BAKING TEMPERATURE:	**350°F (180°C, gas mark 4) convection mode**
BAKING TIME:	**12 to 15 minutes**

This version of brioche mixes the warmth of the spices with the coolness of a sweet pumpkin pastry cream. Some may consider it decadent for breakfast, but everyone can agree that it's perfect for afternoon tea or even for dessert.

Pre-ferment (Biga)

Ingredient	Metric	Weight	Volume	Baker's %
Bread flour	200 g	7.05 oz	1½ cups	100
Whole milk	120 g	4.23 oz	½ cup	60
Instant yeast, preferably osmotolerant	0.5 g	Pinch	Pinch	0.1

Dough

Ingredient	Metric	Weight	Volume	Baker's %
Pumpkin Pastry Cream (page 155)	1 batch	1 batch	1 batch	n/a
Eggs, whole	50 g	1.76 oz	1 egg	9.4
Egg yolks	25 g	0.88 oz	1 yolk	8
Whole milk	16 g	0.56 oz	4 tsp	5
Pumpkin puree**	250 g	8.81 oz	1 cup	75
Honey	33 g	1.16 oz	1½ tbsp	10
Pre-ferment	All of it	All of it	All of it	50
Bread flour or all-purpose flour	330 g	11.64 oz	2½ cups + 2 tbsp	100
Instant yeast, preferably osmotolerant	5 g	0.17 oz	1 tsp	1.5

Dough (continued)

Ingredient	Metric	Weight	Volume	Baker'
Salt	7 g	0.24 oz	1 tsp	2.3
Granulated sugar	43 g	1.51 oz	¼ cup	13
Ground cinnamon	0.6 g	0.02 oz	½ tsp	0.2
Ground nutmeg	0.3 g	0.01 oz	¼ tsp	0.1
Ground ginger	0.3 g	0.01 oz	¼ tsp	0.1
Ground cloves	0.3 g	0.01 oz	¼ tsp	0.1
Unsalted butter	116 g	4 oz	½ cup	35
Egg Wash (page 152)	1 batch	1 batch	1 batch	n/a
Chocolate Glaze (page 151)	1 batch	1 batch	1 batch	n/a
Sliced Almond Crunch (page 156, optional)	1 batch	1 batch	1 batch	n/a
Powdered sugar for topping (optional)	As desired	As desired	As desired	n/a

Procedure:

Day before baking:

1. Combine all of the pre-ferment ingredients in the bowl of a 5-quart (5 L) stand mixer and mix at low speed until a smooth consistency is achieved. This pre-ferment is stiff, so you may need to work it a bit by hand to incorporate all the ingredients. Place in a plastic proofing container sprayed with nonstick cooking spray and cover with lid or plastic wrap. Allow to ferment overnight at room temperature (about 18 hours at 68° to 70°F [20° to 21°C]).

Baking day:

1. Prepare a batch of Pumpkin Pastry Cream, cover with plastic wrap, and refrigerate.

2. Bring the eggs, egg yolks, milk, and pumpkin puree to just under room temperature, about 62°F (17°C), then pour into the bowl of a 5-quart (5 L) stand mixer. Add the honey and the pre-ferment.

3. Add the dry ingredients (flour, instant yeast, salt, granulated sugar, and spices) and mix at low speed to cleanup stage, approximately 4 minutes.

4. While the dough is mixing, take the butter from the refrigerator and make it plastic by hammering it with a rolling pin.

5. Increase the mixing speed to medium and slowly add the butter in stages. Be sure that each stage of butter is completely incorporated into the dough before adding the next portion. Mix the dough until it is well developed and check with a gluten window test. (See page 57.)

6. Work the dough lightly into a round shape and place in a proofing container. Cover and let rest for 1½ hours at room temperature **(a)**.

7. After resting, use a scale to divide the dough into 75 g (2.5 oz) units and preshape into rounds. Cover with plastic wrap and let rest for 20 minutes at room temperature.

8. Final shape the dough rounds and place the brioche on a parchment-lined half sheet pan and place in a protected environment to proof for 45 to 60 minutes.

9. Prepare the Chocolate Glaze.

10. Preheat a convection oven to 350°F (180°C, gas mark 4) about 20 minutes before baking.

11. After the dough has proofed, brush the tops of each domed brioche with Egg Wash and use your hands to open the center and create an indented cavity to hold the filling. Fill the center with about 1 heaping tablespoon [14 g] of Pumpkin Pastry Cream **(b)**.

12. Using a pastry bag or a spoon, apply the Chocolate Glaze to the outer rim of the brioches. If desired, sprinkle with Sliced Almond Crunch before dusting heavily with powdered sugar. This will give a nice crackled effect after baking **(c)**.

13. Bake in the preheated oven for 12 to 15 minutes, until golden brown. Remove from the oven and place the brioches on a wire rack to cool.

Note: Because these brioches are made with components that contain eggs and dairy, they should be refrigerated, if not consumed immediately, for no longer than 24 hours. The quality, texture, and flavor are the best when fresh.

a) **Divide and shape** the dough into small rounds.

b) **Spread open** the center to create a place for the filling.

c) **Pipe the Chocolate Glaze** around the outer edge.

Rum-Raisin-Almond Brioche

YIELD:	**14 to 16 muffin-size brioches**
BAKING TEMPERATURE:	**350°F (180°C, gas mark 4) convection mode**
BAKING TIME:	**18 to 20 minutes**

Juicy rum-soaked raisins meld with the soft almond paste to produce one of the most pleasurable and sophisticated versions of brioche. The source of its inspiration was two of my favorite desserts from childhood: rum-raisin ice cream and chocolate-covered marzipan. It took more than a few attempts to get the right balance of ingredients and flavors, but eventually everything clicked. The brioche bakes up light and buttery with intensely flavored pockets of warm rum raisins and melt-in-your-mouth almond paste—a nice addition to the weekend brunch. Or, serve it as a dessert along with some vanilla-bean ice cream drizzled with the leftover rum syrup—simply divine!

Pre-ferment (Poolish)

Ingredient	Metric	Weight	Volume	Baker's %
Bread flour	165 g	5.82 oz	1⅓ cups	100
Whole milk	165 g	5.82 oz	⅔ cup	100
Instant yeast, preferably osmotolerant	Pinch	Pinch	Pinch	n/a

Dough

Ingredient	Metric	Weight	Volume	Baker's %
Dark raisins	250 g	8.81 oz	2 cups	65.7
Dark rum	100 g	3.52 oz	½ cup	n/a
Simple Syrup (see page 156)	50 g	1.76 oz	¼ cup	n/a
Eggs, whole	100 g	3.52 oz	2 eggs	26.3
Egg yolks	50 g	1.76 oz	2 yolks	13.1
Almond paste	100 g	3.52 oz	½ cup	26.3
Vanilla extract	16 g	0.56 oz	4 tsp	4.2
Pre-ferment	All of it	All of it	All of it	86.8
Bread flour	380 g	13.4 oz	3 cups +	100
Granulated sugar	100 g	3.52 oz	½ cup	26.3

Dough (continued)

Ingredient	Metric	Weight	Volume	Bak
Instant yeast, preferably osmotolerant	8 g	0.28 oz	2 tsp	
Salt	11 g	0.38 oz	2 tsp	
Lemon zest	1 lemon	1 lemon	1 lemon	
Unsalted butter	252 g	8.84 oz	1 cup + 2 tbsp	
Chocolate Glaze (page 151)	1 batch	1 batch	1 batch	
Powdered sugar for topping	As needed	As needed	As needed	

Procedure:

Day before baking:

1. Prepare the poolish: In a plastic container, combine the bread flour, whole milk, and instant yeast until a smooth consistency is achieved. Cover with plastic wrap or lid and allow to stand at room temperature overnight, ideally 12 to 15 hours at 68° to 70°F (20° to 21°C).

2. Soak the dark raisins in the dark rum and add enough Simple Syrup to the container to cover the raisins completely. Allow the raisins to soak overnight at room temperature.

3. Gently roll the almond paste into a small log and cut into ½-inch (1.3 cm) cubes. Place in a lidded container and freeze overnight.

Baking day:

1. Drain the rum-soaked raisins in a colander. *(Note: You can save and store the rum syrup mixture for reuse. Cover and keep in the refrigerator for up to 2 months.)*

2. Spray muffin tins with nonstick cooking spray and set aside.

3. Place the whole eggs, egg yolks, and vanilla in the bowl of a 5-quart (5 L) stand mixer. Scrape the poolish out of its container and add it to the eggs.

4. Add the bread flour, granulated sugar, instant yeast, salt, and lemon zest to the bowl and mix everything at a low speed until cleanup stage.

5. While the dough is mixing, take the butter and hammer it with a rolling pin until it has a plastic quality to it. (See Mixing an Enriched Dough, page 60.)

6. Increase the mixing speed to medium and slowly add the softened butter in stages. After each addition of the butter, mix the dough until the slapping sound subsides and the walls of the mixer are fairly clean.

7. Mix the dough to a full gluten development and check it with a gluten window test. (See page 57.) You should be able to stretch a thin, smooth window without tearing.

8. At this point, add the frozen almond paste chunks and the rum-soaked raisins to the dough and mix at low speed. Stop the mixer periodically to scrape down the bowl sides and dough hook. Mix until the raisins and almond paste are evenly incorporated into the dough.

9. Remove the dough from the mixer and gently preshape into a round. Place in a proofing container, cover, and allow to rest at room temperature for about 2 hours.

10. After this bulk fermentation, use a scale and bench scraper to divide the dough into 100 g (3.5 oz) units (about the size of a small lemon).

11. Work the units round on a floured surface (the soaked raisins tend to make the dough a bit stickier) and place in prepared muffin tins or paper muffin cups **(a)**.

12. Cover the cups with plastic wrap and allow to rest at room temperature until the dough rises to the tops of the muffin cups.

13. During this time, preheat a convection oven to 350°F (180°C, gas mark 4) and mix up a batch of Chocolate Glaze.

14. When the dough has risen to the desired height, use either a piping bag or spoon to spread about 1 tablespoon (14 g) of the Chocolate Glaze on top of each brioche. For a crackled effect, give the tops a heavy dusting of powdered sugar before baking.

15. Place the brioches in the preheated convection oven and bake for 25 minutes, or until golden brown **(b)**.

16. Remove from the oven and let cool in the muffin tins on wire racks. When comfortable to handle, remove from the tins and allow to cool completely.

a) **Place the round units** in the baking cups.

b) **The Rum-Raisin-Almond Brioche:** glazed, dusted, and ready to bake.

Apple Kuchen

YIELD:	**1 half sheet pan**
BAKING TEMPERATURE:	**330°F (165°C, gas mark 3) convection mode**
BAKING TIME:	**30 to 40 minutes**

What could be homier than the flavor of warm, baked apples? How about if they were sautéed in butter with brown sugar and vanilla to give them a sweet, caramel coating, layered on aromatic almond paste, and covered with cinnamon-kissed crumb topping?

This apple kuchen uses the Rum-Raisin-Almond Brioche as the foundation of its formula. Because it is baked in a rimmed sheet pan, it's perfect to take along for a family holiday breakfast or a potluck dessert. It can be served warm, at room temperature, or chilled—my personal favorite is warm with a bit of pure vanilla ice cream on the side!

Ingredient	Metric	Weight	Volume
Rum-Raisin-Almond Brioche (page 106)	1 batch (omit the almond paste)	1 batch (omit the almond paste)	1 batch (omit the almond paste)
Butterkuchen Paste (page 150)	1 batch	1 batch	1 batch
Sautéed Apples (page 156)	1 batch	1 batch	1 batch
Crumb Topping (page 151)	1 batch	1 batch	1 batch
Powdered sugar for topping	As needed	As needed	As needed

Procedure:

Day before baking:

1. Prepare the pre-ferment and the rum-soaked raisins for the Rum-Raisin-Almond Brioche (see page 106.) Do not cube and freeze the almond paste—it is omitted in this version.

2. Mix up a batch of Butterkuchen Paste and refrigerate overnight. *(Note: If you prefer, you can also wait to mix this up on the day of baking.)*

Baking day:

1. Follow the directions for the Rum-Raisin-Almond Brioche and continue to mix up the dough, omitting the addition of the almond paste. When the dough has finished mixing, remove from the mixer and place in a proofing container. Cover and allow to bulk ferment for about 2 hours.

2. During this time, mix up a batch of Butterkuchen Paste, if you did not prepare it the day before. Let the Butterkuchen Paste come to room temperature before placing it in a pastry bag and setting aside.

3. Prepare the Sautéed Apples and set aside.

4. Prepare a batch of Crumb Topping and set aside.

5. After the dough has gone through its bulk fermentation process, place about 1200 to 1300 g (32.3 to 35.8 oz) of the dough in a parchment-lined rimmed sheet pan. With your fingers gently spread out, use the tips of your fingers to "dimple" the dough into the pan, spreading it toward the sides and into the corners. You may need to dimple it once, wait 5 or 10 minutes for the dough to relax, then dimple it again **(a)**.

6. For the leftover dough, prepare some smaller tartlet pans or brioche molds to bake them in. Follow the same instructions as for the larger unit, just bake for less time.

7. Using the pastry bag, pipe 1-inch (2.5 cm) buttons of Butterkuchen Paste all over the surface of the dough, leaving about 1 inch (2.5 cm) of space between the dots. This does not have to be perfect; just evenly distribute the dots. If you do not have a pastry bag, just use 2 spoons as if you were dropping cookie dough onto cookie sheets **(b)**.

8. Add the Sautéed Apples and spread them evenly over the surface of the dough and Butterkuchen Paste **(c)**.

9. Sprinkle the Crumb Topping evenly over the top **(d)**.

10. Cover gently with plastic wrap and allow to proof at room temperature for 1 hour.

11. Preheat a convection oven to 330° to 340°F (165° to 171°C. gas mark 3) about 30 minutes before baking.

12. When the dough is done proofing, place in the preheated convection oven and bake for 30 to 40 minutes. About 15 to 20 minutes into the baking process, nest the sheet pan into an empty one (this is called *double-panning*) to prevent the bottom from getting too brown.

13. Remove from the oven and allow to cool completely in the sheet pan on a wire rack. When completely cool, dust the top with powdered sugar.

a) **Dimple the dough** into the baking form.

b) **Pipe buttons** of Butterkuchen Paste onto the surface.

c) **Place the apples** evenly over the surface.

d) **Sprinkle** crumb topping over the top.

Panettone

YIELD:	**18 mini panettone (3" [7.6 cm] diameter)**
BAKING TEMPERATURE:	**360°F (182°C, gas mark 4) convection mode**
BAKING TIME:	**16 to 18 minutes**

The word *panettone* is derived from the Italian word *panetto*, meaning a small loaf bread—the suffix *-one* changes the meaning to "large bread." This festive bread is widely available and enjoyed for Christmas and New Year's all over the world, but is especially loved in Italy, Latin America, and in certain parts of the United States. Traditionally it has a large, cylindrical base with a domelike top and is made with raisins, and candied orange and lemon peel. Much of its unique flavor comes from an extract called *fiori di sicilia*—an all-natural combination of citrus and vanilla with a pleasingly floral aroma.

This formula makes smaller individual versions of the traditional Panettone—definitely easier to bake and especially nice to have on hand at the holidays for guests or to bring along as a gift for the host of a gala party. For a nice presentation and easy cleanup, remember to order some panettone paper baking cups (see page 168). But don't think you have to wait until December to make it! It's delicious all year round!

Pre-ferment (Biga)

Ingredient	Metric	Weight	Volume	Baker's %
Whole milk	115 g	4 oz	½ cup	60
Instant yeast, preferably osmotolerant	Pinch	Pinch	Pinch	0.1
Bread flour	190 g	6.7 oz	1½ cups	100

Dough

Ingredient	Metric	Weight	Volume	Baker's %
Whole milk	140 g	4.93 oz	½ cup + 1 tbsp	30.1
Egg yolks	150 g	5.29 oz	7 yolks	32.2 oz
Eggs, whole	100 g	3.52 oz	2 eggs	26.3
Fiori di sicilia	4 g	0.14 oz	1 tsp	0.8
Orange blossom water	10 g	0.35 oz	2 tsp	2.1
Pre-ferment	All of it	All of it	All of it	65.5
Bread flour	465 g	16.4 oz	3 ½ cups	100
Malt	5 g	0.17 oz	2 tsp.	1
Granulated sugar	128 g	4.51 oz	⅔ cup	27.5
Salt	9 g	0.31 oz	½ tsp	1.9
Lemon zest	½ lemon	½ lemon	½ lemon	n/a
Unsalted butter	220 g	7.76 oz	1 cup	47.3
Instant yeast, preferably osmotolerant	12 g	0.42 oz	4 tsp	2.5

Dough (continued)

Ingredient	Metric	Weight	Volume	Ba
Golden raisins	200 g	7 oz	1⅔ cups, loosely packed	
Candied lemon peel, diced	60 g	2.11 oz	⅓ cup	
Candied orange peel, diced	80 g	2.82 oz	½ cup	
Crunch topping (optional, page 152)	1 batch	1 batch	1 batch	

Procedure:

Day before baking:

1. Mix the biga: Warm the milk to 70°F (21°C) and pour into a mixing bowl. Add the instant yeast and stir until it completely dissolves. Add the bread flour and blend together to a smooth consistency. Transfer to a plastic container and cover with either a lid or plastic wrap. Allow the mixture to ferment at room temperature overnight (ideally 14 to 16 hours at 68° to 70°F [20° to 21°C]).

Baking day:

1. Warm the milk, egg yolks, eggs, fiori di sicilia, and orange blossom water to about 68°F (20°C) and place in the bowl of a 5-quart (5 L) stand mixer.

2. Add the pre-ferment, bread flour, malt, granulated sugar, salt, instant yeast, and lemon zest and mix at a low speed until the cleanup stage.

3. Take the cold butter and hammer it with a rolling pin to achieve a plastic-like consistency (see page 60).

4. Increase the mixing speed to medium and slowly add the butter to the dough in stages. Be sure that each addition of butter is fully incorporated into the dough before adding the next piece.

5. Mix the dough to a full gluten development and check the dough with a gluten window test. (See page 57.) After the dough is fully developed, add the golden raisins, candied lemon peel, and candied orange peel to the dough and mix until evenly distributed **(a)**. Stop the mixer from time to time to clean the dough hook of fruit and dough.

6. Turn the dough out onto a work surface and preshape into a round (see page 63).

7. Cover the dough with plastic wrap and allow to bulk ferment for about 2 hours.

8. After the bulk fermentation, divide the dough into 90 g (3.2 oz) units using a scale and a bench scraper.

9. Work the units round and place in 2¾-inch (7 cm) paper panettone baking molds. You can also use popover pans or, in a pinch, muffin tins sprayed with nonstick baking spray, but you may have to adjust baking times **(b)**.

10. Cover with plastic wrap and let proof for 2 to 3 hours at about 78°F (26°C). If it is warmer, then your proofing time will be briefer; likewise, if it is colder, you may need more time to proof.

11. Preheat a convection oven to 360°F (182°C, gas mark 4) about 30 minutes before baking.

12. Optional: If desired, prepare a batch of Crunch Topping and top each proofed panettone with a bit just before putting into the oven to bake **(c)**.

13. After the final proof, bake in the preheated convection oven for 16 to 18 minutes. The tops should be golden brown and a nice crown should form over the top of the paper baking mold.

a) **Add the dried fruits** after the dough is fully developed.

b) **Place the round units** in the baking cups.

c) **A tray of panettone** ready for baking.

Stollen ● DVD CONTENT

YIELD:	**5 loaves (500 g [17.6 oz] each)**
BAKING TEMPERATURE:	**340°F (171°C, gas mark 4) convection mode**
BAKING TIME:	**25 to 30 minutes**

This traditional German Christmas bread dates back to the 1400s and has gone through many changes since. Originally it was made without butter, as the pope had banned its use during the fasting time of the Advent season. Thank goodness, this rule was eventually overturned and the stollen evolved to the buttery, flavorful treat it is today.

This version of stollen contains colorful jewel-toned fruits, toasted almonds, and comforting spices. You'll find the traditional flavors (dark

Pre-ferment (Biga)

Ingredient	Metric	Weight	Volume	Baker's %
Bread flour	345 g	12.16 oz	2⅔ cups	100
Whole milk	228 g	8 oz	1 cup	66
Instant yeast, preferably osmotolerant	0.5 g	0.01 oz	Pinch	0.1

Dough

Ingredient	Metric	Weight	Volume	Baker's %
Raisins, dark	250 g	8.81 oz	2 cups	50
Raisins, golden	200 g	7 oz	1⅔ cups	40
Dried cranberries	200 g	7 oz	1⅔ cups	40
Dried apricots ¼-inch (6 mm) cubed	150 g	5.29	1 cup	30
Dark rum	100 g	3.52 oz	½ cup	20
Simple Syrup (page 156)	As needed	As needed	As needed	n/a
Pre-ferment	All of it	All of it	All of it	114.7
Bread flour	500 g	17.63 oz	4 cups	100

Dough (continued)

Ingredient	Metric	Weight	Volume	Bake▸
Whole milk	114 g	4 oz	½ cup	22
Vanilla extract	20 g	0.70 oz	1½ tbsp	4
Whole eggs	150 g	5.29 oz	3 eggs	3
Lemon zest	1 lemon	1 lemon	1 lemon	n/
Granulated sugar	115 g	4 oz	½ cup	2
Instant yeast, preferably osmotolerant	20 g	0.70 oz	2 tbsp	4
Salt	16 g	0.56 oz	2 tsp	3.
Ground cinnamon	3 g	0.1 oz	1½ tsp	0.
Unsalted butter	224 g	7.9 oz	1 cup	44
Slivered almonds	150 g	5.29	1½ cups	3
Almond Paste Filling (page 150)	1 batch	1 batch	1 batch	n/
Unsalted clarified butter* (for glazing)	114 g	4 oz	1 stick	n/
Granulated sugar for topping	As needed	As needed	As needed	n

*See "Making Clarified Butter," page 113.

raisins, cinnamon, and rum) plus some not-so-traditional additions, such as dried cranberries and apricots. Tucked away in the bread is a surprise: a rich almond paste mixture. While it is optional, it is one of my favorite components of the bread—it adds just the right amount of moistness and flavor to the whole experience.

Procedure:

Day before baking:

1. Place all of the biga ingredients in a bowl of a 5-quart (5 L) stand mixer and mix at a low speed, until combined and a smooth consistency is achieved. Transfer to a plastic container, cover, and allow to ferment overnight at room temperature.

2. Place the dark raisins, golden raisins, dried cranberries, and cubed dried apricots in a bowl or container. Add the dark rum and then add enough Simple Syrup to just cover the top of the fruit with liquid. Cover and let the dried fruit macerate at room temperature overnight. *(Note: For a fuller flavor, soak the fruit for up to 1 week in the refrigerator.)*

Baking day:

1. Using a colander or strainer, drain the liquid from the macerated dried fruit. Allow the fruit to sit in the colander or strainer while you mix the dough. *(Note: You can save the drained rum syrup liquid to use later; store covered in the refrigerator for up to 2 months.)*

2. In the bowl of a 5-quart (5 L) stand mixer, combine the pre-ferment, bread flour, milk, vanilla extract, whole eggs, lemon zest, granulated sugar, instant yeast, salt, and ground cinnamon, and mix at a low speed until the dough comes together (about 4 minutes).

3. Take the first portion of unsalted butter (not the clarified butter to be used for glazing) and hammer it with a rolling pin to soften it into a plastic state.

4. Increase the mixing speed to medium and slowly incorporate the butter in stages. Be sure that each addition of butter is fully incorporated into the dough before adding the next portion.

5. Mix the dough to a full gluten development; perform a gluten window test to check the development. (See page 57.) When the dough has reached full development, reduce the mixing speed to low and slowly add the macerated fruit and slivered almonds until evenly incorporated. Periodically stop the mixer to scrape down the bowl sides and dough hook.

6. Turn out the dough onto a lightly floured work surface and loosely shape into a smooth, round ball. Place in an oiled proofing container, cover, and allow to bulk ferment for 1½ to 2 hours.

7. Using a scale and bench scraper, divide the dough into 400 to 500 g (14.1 to 17.6 oz) units and work into a round. Cover with plastic wrap and let rest for an additional 20 minutes.

8. Mix up a batch of Almond Paste Filling and set aside.

9. Uncover the dough and shape each dough unit into a torpedo shape. Using a wooden dowel or thin rolling pin, press down in the center to make a trough down the middle of the dough. Gently roll the dowel back and forth a bit to create a thinner section of dough about 6 inches (15.2 cm) wide between the two fatter dough sections (a, b, c).

Continued on page 114

Making CLARIFIED BUTTER

Place a stick of unsalted butter in a small saucepan and melt on low heat. Allow to simmer for 20 to 30 minutes, until all the milk solids have separated out of the liquid. Skim off the foam at the top with a spoon, then pour the butter through a strainer to remove the solids. Store this clarified butter in the refrigerator until ready to use, then melt as necessary.

Stollen (continued)

10. Divide the Almond Paste Filling into five even portions and roll out into a 1-inch (2.5 cm) -diameter log. Lay the log on top of the thin dough. Take one of the fat dough sections and bring it over the almond paste log and nestle it down between the log and the other section of dough. Cover and allow to proof for about 1 hour, or until doubled in size **(d)**.

11. Preheat a convection oven to 340°F (171°C, gas mark 4) about 30 minutes before baking.

12. After final proof, bake in the preheated convection oven for 25 to 30 minutes. The stollen should develop a nice golden brown color. While it is baking, melt the clarified unsalted butter reserved for glazing. (If you haven't clarified the butter already, then let it sit for a minute and then skim off the solids on the top with spoon or a strainer.)

13. Remove the stollen from the oven and while it is still hot, brush the surface with the clarified butter. Immediately coat generously with granulated sugar. Place on a wire rack to cool completely overnight **(e)**.

14. Dust generously with powdered sugar.

The fruit as it is mixed into the dough.

a) **Roll the center** out thinly.

b) **Set** the almond paste log in the dough.

c) **Fold over** the dough to cover.

d) **The stollen is placed** to proof on a parchment-lined sheet pan.

e) **Brush the stollen** with clarified butter and toss in granulated sugar.

Gibassier ● DVD CONTENT

YIELD: **12 individual loaves**
BAKING TEMPERATURE: **350°F (180°C, gas mark 4) convection mode**
BAKING TIME: **10 to 12 minutes**

This little-known breakfast bread hails from the Provence region in France and is, in my wife's opinion, one of the best breakfast breads ever to have graced our table. She is not alone; most everyone that has been lucky enough to taste a gibassier falls in love instantly. Perhaps it is the light, buttery texture or the aroma of orange blossom water mixed with the delicate hint of aniseed. Whatever it is, this little baked gem has the potential for a cultlike following among bakers everywhere. While this may be your chance to be at the forefront of a baking obsession, beware—one bite may inspire you to quit your day job and travel the country as a self-proclaimed gibassier ambassador, extolling the virtues of this marvelous bread to anyone within earshot. Okay…maybe that's just a little far-fetched. Perhaps a trip to your local library for *A Year in Provence* will do the trick instead (along with a little gibassier, of course!).

Pre-ferment (Biga)

Ingredient	Metric	Weight	Volume	Baker's %
Bread flour	180 g	6.34 oz	1½ cups	100
Whole milk	110 g	3.88 oz	½ cup	61.1
Instant yeast, preferably osmotolerant	0.03 g	0.01 oz	Pinch	0.1

Dough

Ingredient	Metric	Weight	Volume	Baker's %
Eggs, whole	130 g	4.58 oz	2 eggs + 1 yolk	32.5
Olive oil	65 g	2.29 oz	⅓ cup	16.2
Orange blossom water	38 g	1.34 oz	7½ tbsp	9.5
Water	25 g	0.88 oz	2 tbsp	6.2
Bread flour	400 g	14.1 oz	3¼ cups	100
Pre-ferment	All of it	All of it	All of it	72.5
Granulated sugar	100 g	3.52 oz	½ cup	25
Salt	7 g	0.24 oz	1 tsp	1.7

Dough (continued)

Ingredient	Metric	Weight	Volume	Baker's %
Instant yeast, preferably osmotolerant	10 g	0.35 oz	2 tsp	2.5
Unsalted butter	70 g	2.46 oz	5 tbsp	17.5
Aniseed	6 g	0.21 oz	1½ tsp	1.5
Candied orange peel, ¼" (6 mm) cubed	70 g	2.46 oz	½ cup	17.5
Granulated sugar for topping	As needed	As needed	As needed	n/a
Clarified butter	113 g	4 oz.	½ cup	n/a

Procedure:

Day before baking:

1. Combine all the pre-ferment ingredients in the bowl of a 5-quart (5 L) stand mixer and mix at low speed until a smooth consistency is achieved. Remove from the bowl and place in an oiled plastic proofing container and cover with a lid or plastic wrap. Allow to stand overnight (14 to 16 hours) at room temperature.

Baking day:

1. Before starting, bring the eggs, olive oil, orange blossom water, and water to about 60°F (15.5°C). The best way to do this is to place the liquid ingredients in a microwave oven and heat in 15-second intervals, stirring and checking the temperature after every heat application.

2. In the bowl of a 5-quart (5 L) stand mixer, pour in the warmed liquids, add the pre-ferment, and then add the bread flour, granulated sugar, salt, and instant yeast. Using a dough hook, mix together at low speed until the dough comes together (about 4 minutes).

3. Increase the mixing speed to medium and mix for an additional 4 minutes.

4. In the meantime, soften the unsalted butter to a plastic state by hammering it with a rolling pin. (See page 60.)

5. Slowly add the softened butter to the mixing dough in stages. Be sure that each portion of butter is completely incorporated into the dough before adding the next portion.

6. Mix the dough until the dough is fully developed. Check the gluten development by performing a gluten window test. (See page 57.)

7. When the dough is fully developed, reduce the mixing speed to low and add the aniseed and candied orange peel. Stop the mixer periodically to scrape the dough off the hook. Continue to mix until the fruit and seeds are evenly distributed. This usually takes about 2 minutes, scraping down the hook about 3 times.

a) **Cover the round units** with plastic wrap and let rest.

b) **Gently press** the torpedo-shaped dough flat and make the cuts into the dough.

8. Turn the dough out onto a work surface and lightly shape into a round. Place in an oil-sprayed plastic container and cover with plastic wrap, and let bulk ferment for 1½ to 2 hours (a).

9. Using a scale and a bench scraper, divide the dough into 90 or 100 g (3.2 or 3.5) units and work into rounds, then cover and let rest for about 20 minutes.

10. Shape the dough units into torpedoes and then use your hand to gently press them flat. They should be shaped somewhat like a half circle (b).

11. Place the straighter edge of the dough near to you and use a 2-inch (5 cm) -wide putty knife (a clean one, of course!) to cut three slits completely through the dough: one in the center "noon" position and the other two at "ten thirty" and "one thirty." Next, cut four ¾-inch (1.9 cm) -long slits into the outer edge of the dough, splitting the difference in between the major slits so that you end up with 4 cuts along the outer edge of the dough.

12. Pick up each unit, open it with a gentle stretch, and place it on a parchment-lined sheet pan. Let the units proof, covered with plastic wrap, for about 1 to 1½ hours (c).

13. Preheat a convection oven to 350°F (180°C, gas mark 4) about 30 minutes before baking. Prepare the clarified butter (see page 113).

14. After proofing, place the sheet pan in the preheated convection oven and bake for 10 to 12 minutes, or until golden brown.

15. Remove from the oven and brush the hot gibassiers with clarified butter. After the butter has set, toss the gibassiers in granulated sugar while still warm, then set on a wire rack to cool (d).

c) **Open the cut dough units** with a gentle stretch to reveal the shape.

d) **Brush with clarified butter** and toss in granulated sugar.

Bostock

YIELD: **varies**

BAKING TEMPERATURE: **350°F (180°C, gas mark 4) convection mode**

BAKING TIME: **12 to 15 minutes**

What began in Europe as a way for bakers to use day-old or stale brioches became such a beloved treat they had to start baking more brioches just to keep up with the demand. And no wonder—who could resist a slice of brioche spread with an almond cream paste and sprinkled with sliced almonds, all baked to golden perfection? Although it is typically made using the traditional brioche, you can easily try any of the other enriched dough breads in this chapter. And if you don't have any of those on hand or in the freezer, here's a secret: You can always dress up a good-quality store-bought loaf, too.

Ingredient	Metric	Weight	Volume
Bostock Syrup (page 150)	1 batch	1 batch	1 batch
Almond Bostock Paste	1 batch	1 batch	1 batch
Brioche loaf	1 to 2	1 to 2	1 to 2
Sliced Almond Crunch (page 156)	As desired	As desired	As desired
Powdered sugar	As desired	As desired	As desired

Procedure:

Day before baking:

1. Prepare a batch of the Bostock Syrup by soaking orange slices in the water/sugar/corn syrup mixture; cover and refrigerate overnight. Prepare a batch of Almond Bostock Paste and refrigerate overnight (**a**).

Baking day:

1. Preheat a convection oven to 350°F (180°C, gas mark 4) about 30 minutes before baking.

2. Remove the Bostock Syrup and Almond Bostock Paste from the refrigerator. Slice a brioche loaf into ¾-inch (1.9 cm) -thick slices (**b**). Using a pastry brush, lightly coat both sides of each side with some syrup and place them on a wire rack over a sheet pan (**c**).

3. Use an offset spatula or knife to evenly spread about 2 tablespoons (28 g) of Almond Bostock Paste onto the top of each slice **(d)**. If the paste is too firm to easily spread, warm it up a bit in a microwave until it is soft enough to spread. Sprinkle a bit of the Sliced Almond Crunch on top and dust with powdered sugar before baking **(e, f)**.

4. Place the bostock on a parchment-lined half sheet pan and bake for 12 to 15 minutes. The paste should have a light golden, toasted color.

5. Remove from the oven and place on a wire rack to cool. Serve slightly warm or at room temperature and enjoy immediately on the day of baking.

a) **Soak oranges** to flavor the syrup.

b) **Slice a loaf** of brioche or other enriched bread.

b) **Lightly coat** each side with syrup and place on wire rack..

d) **Spread on** the Almond Bostock Paste.

e) **Sprinkle with** Sliced Almond Crunch.

f) **Dust with** powdered sugar.

Basic Sweet Dough

YIELD: **Refer to variation**

BAKING TEMPERATURE: **Refer to variation**

BAKING TIME: **Refer to variation**

Every baker needs a tried-and-true sweet dough formula that is versatile and dependable—one that is made from simple ingredients and is easy to make. Whether you are craving melt-in-your-mouth sticky buns or something more formal and decorative, like a Russian braid or glazed tea ring, this Basic Sweet Dough formula will be the one you turn to for years. The entire dough is mixed the day before baking, which makes it great when you are coordinating active work time in your kitchen, particularly when it involves any kind of holiday or special event.

Procedure:

Day before baking:

1. Bring the whole milk and eggs to room temperature. (Optional: Split the vanilla bean in half lengthwise, scrape out the seeds, and add the seeds to the milk.) If you are taking the ingredients directly from the refrigerator and would like to speed up the process, you can place them in a microwavable container and microwave in 10-second intervals, stirring between heating sessions. Stop when the temperature is about 68°F (20°C).

2. Pour the liquids into the bowl of a 5-quart (5 L) stand mixer. Add the bread flour, instant yeast, sugar, salt, malt, and lemon zest. Mix at low speed until the dough comes together (cleanup stage). Scrape the dough down off the hook from time to time if necessary.

Ingredient	Metric	Weight	Volume	Baker's %
Whole milk	365 g	12.87 oz	1½ cups	55.3
Eggs, whole	50 g	1.76 oz	1 egg	7.5
Vanilla bean (optional)	½ bean	½ bean	½ bean	n/a
Bread flour	660 g	23.28 oz	5¼ cups	100
Instant yeast, preferably osmotolerant	13 g	0.45 oz	3 tsp	1.9
Granulated sugar	70 g	2.46 oz	⅓ cup	10.6
Salt	13 g	0.45 oz	1½ tsp	1.9
Malt, diastatic (see page 121)	7 g	0.24 oz	2 tsp	1
Lemon zest	½ lemon	½ lemon	½ lemon	n/a
Unsalted butter	70 g	2.46 oz	5 tbsp	10.6

All about MALT

Malt is used by many professional bakers and comes in two types: diastatic and nondiastatic. Both are made from sprouted grains (usually barley) that have been dried and ground, but only the diastatic malt contains natural active enzymes. These enzymes help to break down the starch to make sugars for the yeast to feed on. Sweet enriched doughs that go through a longer, cold fermentation process benefit from the extra food available to the yeast. If the yeast has enough food, then it grows actively during the fermentation process, resulting in a better rise and flavor. Second, these extra sugars caramelize during the baking process and help to build a nice crispy brown crust, which looks nice and helps improve the shelf life of the bread. Because most commercially available flours have a small percentage of malt added to them, this additional boost of malt is a personal choice and considered an optional ingredient. Diastatic malt improves the performance, but is not absolutely necessary.

3. Soften the butter to a plastic stage by hammering it with a rolling pin. Increase the mixing speed to medium and slowly add the softened butter in stages. Make sure you give each addition of butter enough time to fully incorporated into the dough before adding the next.

4. When the dough is fully developed (check with a gluten window test; see page 57), place the dough in a plastic container sprayed with oil, cover, and allow to bulk ferment for 2 hours at room temperature.

5. After the bulk fermentation, place on a sheet pan lined with parchment and press the dough down to about ¾ inch (1.9 cm) thick. This ensures a quick, uniform cooling process for the dough. Cover the dough with plastic wrap and place in the refrigerator overnight.

Baking day:

1. Remove the dough from the refrigerator. Choose one of the variations and follow the respective shaping and baking instructions.

Two of the tempting sweet dough variations: Tea Ring, page 126 (left) and Russian Braid, page 128 (right)

Pecan Sticky Buns

YIELD:	**12 to 14 buns**
BAKING TEMPERATURE:	**350°F (180°C, gas mark 4) convection mode**
BAKING TIME:	**15 to 18 minutes**

Procedure:

Day before baking:

1. Prepare a batch of Cinnamon Bun Filling (can be made up to 1 week in advance). Prepare a batch of Sticky Bun Smear (can be made up to 1 week in advance). For best results, mix a little bit of Egg Wash for sealing the dough (although plain water can also be used.)

2. Prepare the muffin tins: spray each with some nonstick cooking spray and place about 1 tablespoon (14 g) of Sticky Bun Smear in the bottom of each impression, pressing it down with your fingers. Arrange 3 pecan halves upside down on top of the smear. Place the muffin tins on a sheet pan and set aside **(a)**.

Baking day:

1. Remove the dough from the refrigerator, unwrap the plastic, and place the dough on a lightly floured surface. Use a rolling pin to roll out the dough 16 inches (40.5 cm) wide and just under ¼ inch (6 mm) thick (the length will be determined by these two dimensions).

2. Spread a thin layer of filling over the entire surface of the dough, leaving a 1-inch (2.5 cm) strip free along one long side.

3. Brush the plain dough edge with a bit of egg wash. Starting with the long end that is covered with filling (opposite the egg-washed edge), roll up the dough evenly into a long log and seal the edge to the log **(b)**.

Ingredient	Metric	Weight	Volume
Cinnamon Bun Filling (page 151)	1 batch	1 batch	1 batch
Sticky Bun Smear (page 157)	1 batch	1 batch	1 batch
Egg Wash (page 152)	As needed	As needed	As needed
Pecan halves	36 to 42	36 to 42	36 to 42
Basic Sweet Dough (page 120)	1 batch	1 batch	1 batch

4. Use a sharp knife to cut the log into 1½-inch (3.8 cm) sections **(c)**. Place each section on end in a muffin cup **(d)**. Cover with plastic wrap and let proof at room temperature for about 45 minutes to 1 hour. The dough should approximately double in size.

5. Preheat a convection oven to 350°F (180°C, gas mark 4) about 30 minutes before baking.

6. After proofing, place in the preheated convection oven and bake for 15 to 18 minutes.

7. Remove from the oven and place the muffin tins on a wire rack for about 2 minutes to set up. Then, take another sheet pan and place it upside down on the tops of the buns. Grab both the top and bottom sheet pans at once and turn them over to invert the buns and release them from the muffin tins. Let them cool to room temperature and then enjoy!

Are your STICKY BUNS STICKING?

When you remove the buns from the oven, let them sit for a couple of minutes to give the melted sugars some time to set up—if you don't, the syrup will leak everywhere. On the other hand, if you find that you've waited too long and the sugars have set too much, preventing the buns from releasing from the tins, just heat them in the oven for a few minutes to help them release.

a) **Press the Sticky Bun Smear** into the muffin tins and arrange pecan halves on top.

b) **Roll up the dough** and filling to create a log.

c) **Cut the log** into sections.

d) **Place each unit** in a muffin cup.

Sweet Glazed Cinnamon Buns

YIELD:	**12 to 14 buns**
BAKING TEMPERATURE:	**350°F (180°C, gas mark 4) convection mode**
BAKING TIME:	**15 to 18 minutes**

Ingredient	Metric	Weight	Volume
Cinnamon Bun Filling (page 151)	1 batch	1 batch	1 batch
Sugar Glaze (page 157)	1 batch	1 batch	1 batch
Egg Wash (page 152)	As needed	As needed	As needed
Basic Sweet Dough (page 120)	1 batch	1 batch	1 batch

Procedure:

1. Prepare a batch of Cinnamon Bun Filling (can be made up to 1 week in advance). Prepare a batch of Sugar Glaze. Mix a little bit of Egg Wash for sealing the dough.

2. These can be made in either muffin tins or on a sheet pan. To prepare muffin tins: spray each with nonstick cooking spray. To prepare a sheet pan: spray a parchment-lined sheet pan with nonstick cooking spray.

3. Remove the dough from the refrigerator, unwrap the plastic, and place the dough onto a lightly floured surface. Use a rolling pin to roll out the dough 16 inches (40.5 cm) wide and just under ¼ inch (6 mm) thick (the length will be determined by these two dimensions).

4. Spread a thin layer of filling over the entire surface of the dough, except leave 1 inch (2.5 cm) of a long end free of filling **(a)**.

5. Brush the plain dough edge with a bit of egg wash. Starting with the long end that is covered with filling (opposite the egg-washed edge), roll up the dough evenly into a long log and seal the edge to the log.

6. Use a sharp knife to cut the roll into 1½-inch (3.8 cm) -long sections. Place each section on end into a muffin cup. Or, place them on end on a sheet pan about 1 inch (2.5 cm) apart from each other. Cover and let proof at room temperature for about 45 minutes to 1 hour. The dough should approximately double in size **(b)**.

7. Preheat a convection oven to 350°F (180°C, gas mark 4) about 30 minutes before baking.

8. After proofing, place in the preheated convection oven and bake for 15 to 18 minutes, or until golden brown on top.

9. Remove the buns from the oven and spoon or brush the Sugar Glaze over the tops immediately while still hot from the oven. Let them cool to room temperature and then enjoy!

a) **Spread the filling** and roll up the dough.

b) **Place the sections** on a sheet pan or into muffin cups and let proof.

Tea Ring

YIELD:	**1 ring**
BAKING TEMPERATURE:	**340°F (171°C, gas mark 4) convection mode**
BAKING TIME:	**25 to 30 minutes**

Procedure:

1. Prepare a batch of Cinnamon Bun Filling or Hazelnut Filling (can be made up to 1 week in advance.) Prepare a batch of Sugar Glaze either now or during the baking process. Cover the glaze with the plastic wrap directly touching the surface to prevent a crust from forming. Mix a little bit of Egg Wash for sealing the dough.

2. Spray a parchment-lined sheet pan with some nonstick cooking spray and set aside.

3. Remove the dough from the refrigerator, unwrap the plastic, and place the dough on a lightly floured surface. Use a rolling pin to roll out the dough 16 inches (40.5 cm) wide and just under ¼ inch (6 mm) thick (the length will be determined by these two dimensions).

4. Spread a thin layer of filling over the entire surface of the dough, except leave 1 inch (2.5 cm) of a long end free of filling.

5. Brush the plain dough edge with a bit of egg wash. Starting with the long end that is covered with filling (opposite the egg-washed edge), roll up the dough evenly into a long log and seal the edge to the log **(a)**.

6. To make the tea ring, gently pull one end of the log to create a dull point and push an indentation into the other end of the log, then curve the log into a ring and press the ends together into each other **(b)**.

Ingredient	Metric	Weight	Volume
Cinnamon Bun Filling (page 151) or Hazelnut Filling (page 154)	1 batch	1 batch	1 batch
Sugar Glaze (page 157)	1 batch	1 batch	1 batch
Egg Wash (page 152)	As needed	As needed	As needed
Basic Sweet Dough (page 120)	1 batch	1 batch	1 batch
Chopped nuts as garnish (optional)	As desired	As desired	As desired

7. Place the ring on the prepared parchment-lined sheet pan and, using a pair of kitchen scissors, make 1-inch (2.5 cm) -long slices three-quarters of the way into the dough around the entire ring (c). Take each section and twist slightly to expose the center, overlapping them as you work around the ring (d). Cover and let proof at room temperature for about 45 minutes to 1 hour. The dough should approximately double in size.

8. Preheat a convection oven to 340°F (171°C, gas mark 4) about 30 minutes before baking.

9. After proofing, place in the preheated convection oven and bake for 25 to 30 minutes.

10. Remove the tea ring from the oven and spoon or brush the Sugar Glaze over the top immediately while still hot from the oven (e). Sprinkle with chopped nuts if desired. Let cool to room temperature and then enjoy!

RINGS of all sizes

This tea ring is so pretty and decorative, you may want to make one for yourself and one to give as a gift. The size is easily varied, so don't be afraid to make a couple of smaller rings—or even a small ring with a few cinnamon buns from the leftover dough as an added treat!

a) **Brush the edge** with egg wash before rolling up the dough.

b) **Press the ends together** to form a ring.

c) **Cut 1-inch (2.5 cm) sections** around the entire ring.

d) **Twist each section** to expose the center.

e) **Brush on the Sugar Glaze** while the tea ring is still warm.

Russian Braid

YIELD:	**1 loaf (9" x 4" x 3" (22.9 x 10.2 x 7.6]) plus some extra cinnamon buns**
BAKING TEMPERATURE:	**325°F (170°C, gas mark 3) convection mode**
BAKING TIME:	**40 to 45 minutes**

Procedure:

1. Prepare a batch of Nut Filling (can be made up to 1 week in advance). Prepare a batch of Sugar Glaze either now or during the baking process. Cover the glaze with the plastic wrap directly touching the surface to prevent a crust from forming. Mix up a little bit of Egg Wash.

2. Spray a loaf pan with some nonstick cooking spray and set aside.

3. Remove the dough from the refrigerator, unwrap the plastic, and place the dough on a lightly floured surface. Use a rolling pin to roll out the dough 16-inches (40.5 cm) wide and just under ¼-inch (6 mm) thick (the length will be determined by these two dimensions).

4. Spread a thin layer of filling over the entire surface of the dough, except leave 1 inch (2.5 cm) of a long end free of filling (pistachio nut filling is shown here).

5. Brush the plain dough edge with a bit of egg wash. Starting with the long end that is covered with filling (opposite the egg-washed edge), roll up the dough evenly into a long log and seal the edge to the roll (a).

6. For each loaf pan, cut a section of the log 2-inches (5 cm) longer than the length of the pan. Take a sharp chef's knife and slice the log in half lengthwise to expose the ribboned layers of filling and dough. Line up the two sections side by side with the exposed layers on top, then gently twist them together 2 or 3 times, keeping the exposed layers on top (b).

Ingredient	Metric	Weight	Volume
Nut Filling (page 154)	1 batch	1 batch	1 batch
Sugar Glaze (page 157)	1 batch	1 batch	1 batch
Egg Wash (page 152)	As needed	As needed	As needed
Basic Sweet Dough (page 120)	1 batch	1 batch	1 batch
Chopped nuts as garnish (optional)	As desired	As desired	As desired

7. Place the twisted strands in the prepared loaf pan. Cover and let proof at room temperature for at least 1 hour. The dough should approximately double in size.

8. Preheat a convection oven to 325°F (170°C, gas mark 3) about 30 minutes before baking.

9. After proofing, place in the preheated convection oven and bake for about 40 to 45 minutes. Touch the top of the loaf (be careful not to get burned) to check if it is done. The loaf should be firm and dark brown in color. If it gets too dark too quickly, reduce the temperature of the oven.

10. Remove from the oven, take the braid out of the loaf pan, and place on a wire rack. Spoon or brush the Sugar Glaze over the top immediately while still hot from the oven. Sprinkle with chopped nuts if desired. Let cool to room temperature and then enjoy!

Going a LITTLE NUTTY

If you feel like adding flavor and extra protein to your baking, then nut flours are one way to do it. Nut flours can also be used for dredging meat, poultry, or fish before cooking. They are the key ingredient to nut pastes and fillings and are easy to make at home in a food processor. Hazelnuts, almonds, and pistachios are best; walnuts and pecans have higher fat contents and are more challenging to grind into flour.

Process or pulse frozen or refrigerated nuts in small batches in a food processor. The nuts must be cold, since their high oil content leads to a transition from flour to nut butter. Keep the pulsing sessions short and check the nuts often. Once you have a relatively fine powder, store the nut flour in an airtight container in the freezer to prevent spoiling.

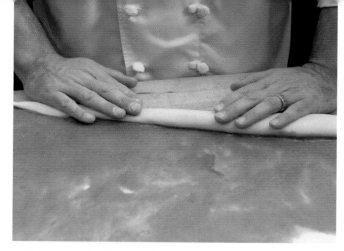

a) **Roll up the dough** and seal the edge.

b) **Split the log in half** lengthwise.

c) **Gently twist** the sections together.

CHAPTER SIX

Laminated Dough

HISTORICALLY, *LAMINATE* ORIGINATES FROM THE LATIN WORD *LAMINA*, meaning "thin piece of metal or wood." More etymologic research reveals one of the earliest uses of the verb translates to "to beat or roll into thin plates"—which is exactly what we do when we make laminated dough. Alternate layers of dough and fat are repeatedly rolled out and folded together to create a multitude of layers.

Laminated doughs encompass many products. Some, such as puff pastry dough, do not require yeast and utilize the leavening power of steam alone to build their layers. But many pastries benefit from the power of yeast, and all the laminated doughs in this book are yeasted. You will find the knowledge crosses over to non-yeasted laminated doughs, should you decide to explore them later.

I am not going to pretend that the process of making a laminated dough is a breeze. A novice baker can still tackle these formulas and succeed, but it definitely takes a certain amount of commitment and patience (and a little muscle along with some experience doesn't hurt, either). Striking the right balance between the delicate butter and yeasted dough does take some finesse and practice to master. All that being said, there is nothing more gratifying than making your own laminated dough and relishing the results. Once you have had the experience of biting through the flaky layers of your own buttery croissant (still warm from the oven), your senses will awaken to the delicate flavors that a great laminated dough imparts. Pastries that you used to be able to consume without a second thought will be scrutinized with a more critical palate. And even if you first create less than Olympic-caliber products, just going through the process will give you an appreciation for the work that goes into making even the seemingly simple (but oh-so-ever complex) croissant.

Because laminated doughs are so time-consuming, I am also including a preparation time to help in your planning. This chapter presents three versatile formulas that make a multitude of products, so roll up your sleeves and get ready to roll out some dough!

Laminated Dough Techniques

The first steps in successfully reproducing the formulas in this chapter are to understand both the structure of laminated dough and the techniques involved in its creation. Laminated products, such as croissants and Danish, are famous for their buttery, flaky layers. But just how does one attain the seemingly endless strata? And perhaps more importantly, what's the point?

If you recall from chapter 1, the three leavening gases in baking are steam, air, and carbon dioxide. Of these, yeasted laminated doughs use two: steam and carbon dioxide (CO_2). During the fermentation process of a yeasted dough, carbon dioxide is produced and provides the rise (or leavening) in the dough. The leavening agent of steam comes from two sources: the water content in the dough and the water present in the layer of butter. When baked, the water from both sources evaporates into steam and the steam travels up and out of the product. The layers of fat separate the layers of dough and prevent them from sticking together, and the pressure from the steam lifts and separates these layers of dough as it travels out toward the surface. And so, flaky layers are born.

A common misconception is that the water from the butter causes this lift. While this source of water contributes to the lift, the majority of the steam comes from the dough. Just look at the moisture content of each: butter (typically used by artisan bakers in laminated doughs) contains approximately 17 percent water, while the dough contains approximately 60 percent moisture. And what about a laminated dough made with shortening (gasp!), a common cost-cutting approach taken by larger mass-producing bakeries? Shortening is 100 percent fat with no moisture, but still can produce a flaky laminated dough. Now that you understand the function of the layers of fat, let's dive into the dough basics and the laminating process. Before you can laminate, you need to do two things: mix a dough and prepare a butter block. The dough that is used is not considered an enriched dough, although technically it does contain butter. Butter is necessary to help prevent the gluten from overdeveloping in the early stages. Ideally the dough builds most of its strength and gluten development during the laminating process rather than in the mixing phase. You mix the dough as you would any other dough, allowing it to go through the bulk fermentation at room temperature. Loosely shape the dough into a rectangular form and transfer it to a parchment-lined sheet pan, then cover with plastic wrap before placing in the refrigerator overnight. This cold fermentation process slows down the yeast fermentation, but the lactic acid bacteria (present in flour and yeast) are still active and contribute a different flavor to the dough.

Place the dough in a sheet pan and cover with plastic wrap before refrigerating.

You also need to prepare what is known to bakers as a butter block, which really isn't a thick block of butter; rather, a neat rectangular sheet. This is the original source of fat sandwiched between the dough. The whole package will then go through a rolling and folding series, creating layers upon layers, each one getting subsequently thinner. The butter block is made to be the same width but only half the length of the dough when it is first rolled out.

MAKING A BUTTER BLOCK DVD CONTENT

To make a butter block for any of the following formulas, first scale out the butter, place it on parchment paper, and soften it by hammering it to a flat rectangle about ⅜ inch (9 mm) thick with a rolling pin. Use a dough divider to trim the edges of the dough straight and use the trimmings to fill in any areas lacking in butter. The goal is to make a neat 5 x 7-inch (12.7 x 17.8 cm) rectangle. Next, cut a piece of parchment paper 13 x 18 inches (33 x 45.7 cm), fold it in half like a book, and crease it. Open up the paper and place the butter on the parchment paper so that the long side of the butter lines up with the crease, then fold the other half on top. Fold in each of the remaining three sides of the parchment paper about 2½ inches (6.3 cm), creating an envelope around the butter block. Turn over the envelope so that the folded edges face the table. Using a rolling pin, roll the butter toward the edges so that the butter completely fills the envelope. You should end up with a rectangular package of butter about 6 x 8 inches (15.2 x 20.3 cm) in size. Place the packaged butter block in the refrigerator overnight.

MAKING A BUTTER BLOCK

a) **Soften the butter** by hammering it with a rolling pin.

b) **Place the butter** onto parchment paper, and shape the entire amount into a rectangle.

c) **Fold up the edges** of the parchment paper to create an envelope around the butter.

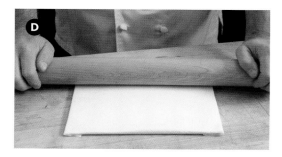

d) **Use a rolling pin** to roll the butter from the center to the edges to create an even rectangular block.

EUROPEAN vs. AMERICAN-STYLE BUTTER

European style butter has a slightly higher butterfat content than its American counterpart (82 versus 80 percent). When you hammer the butter to make it soft, you'll find that European butter becomes nice and soft and pliable, whereas American butter tends to crack and crumble.

An alternative way to make a butter block with American butter is to work it in a stand mixer with a paddle attachment until softened (but do not cream), then add 2 teaspoons (6 g) of flour and mix in. The flour will help absorb the extra moisture and enable the butter block to stay intact during the lamination process. After it has been mixed, proceed with creating the parchment paper envelope and rolling out the butter into the edges. Place it in the refrigerator overnight to allow it to set up

The next day when you are ready to start the laminating process, remove the dough from the refrigerator and place it in the freezer for 30 to 45 minutes. In the meantime, take the butter block out of the refrigerator and, while still in the parchment envelope, soften it by hammering the packet with a rolling pin. It should be the same pliability and consistency as the dough will be before starting the lamination. To check the pliability, run the envelope of butter over the edge of a table or countertop; it should give willingly to the edge and not crack or break.

MAKING A TRIFOLD DVD CONTENT

Remove the dough from the freezer and roll out to a 16 x 8-inch (40.6 x 20.3 cm) rectangle. Remove the butter block from the envelope and place in the center of the dough with the short ends of the butter in line with the long ends of the dough. Fold in the two edges of the dough so that they meet in the middle and press the seam together with your hands.

On a lightly floured surface, roll out the dough lengthwise until it is about ½ inch (1.3 cm) thick. Trim the short ends so that they are straight (use a ruler and pastry wheel). Take a short end of the dough and fold it up two thirds of the way onto itself, then fold the remaining third of the dough on top. This is known as a *trifold*.

Now place the dough on a lightly floured surface in front of you (short end to you) and roll out the dough lengthwise to ½ inch (1.3 cm) thick. Give it another trifold. Place the dough on a sheet pan, cover with plastic wrap, and return to the freezer to rest for 30 minutes. After resting, remove the dough from the freezer and give it one final series of rolling and trifolding. You will now have created 27 layers of butter and dough—great job!

With these foundation laminated dough principles and techniques out of the way, we can now move onward to the different doughs and formulas.

MAKING A TRIFOLD

a) **Place the butter block** into the center of the dough and fold the edges over to meet in the middle.

b) **Press** the seam together.

c) **Use a rolling pin** to roll out the dough lengthwise until it is about ½" (1.3 cm) thick.

d) **Trim the short edges** straight with a sharp knife or pastry wheel.

e) **Fold one short end of the dough** up two thirds of the way onto itself, and then fold the remaining third of the dough on top to create a trifold.

Put a Little BANG in your BUTTER

Who says laminated dough has to be made with plain unsalted butter? Add a little flavor by sprinkling herbs or spices over the butter block before the lamination process begins. Cinnamon, nutmeg, or cardamom for the sweeter side; garlic salt, Italian herbs, or red crushed pepper to spice things up.

All-Purpose Danish

YIELD:	**varies, depending on product**
BAKING TEMPERATURE:	**350°F (180°C, gas mark 4) convection mode**
BAKING TIME:	**15 to 18 minutes on average, but will vary with size and product**
TOTAL TIME:	**32 hours over 3 days (1 hour total of active work)**

This dough formula is one of my all-time favorites. Although it requires a few days of preparation, you'll welcome the range of products that can be made with this dough. From sweet to savory, this dough can assume many different roles at the table. It pairs just as well with pastry cream and fruit toppings as it does with a spinach cheese filling. Once laminated, this dough can be frozen for up to a week. This makes it easy to defrost smaller portions at different times during the week. (One day, enjoy a fruit Danish for breakfast, while another day make Parmesan pinwheels to accompany dinner.)

Dough

Ingredient	Metric	Weight	Volume	Baker's %
Whole milk	310 g	10.93 oz	1¼ cups	44.9
Bread flour	690 g	24.33 oz	5½ cups	100
Eggs, whole	100 g	3.52 oz	2 eggs	14.9
Granulated sugar	80 g	2.82 oz	⅓ cup	11.5
Salt	13 g	0.45 oz	1½ tsp	1.8
Instant yeast	9 g	0.31 oz	2 tsp	1.3
Unsalted butter	28 g	0.98 oz	2 tbsp	4

Butter Block

Ingredient	Metric	Weight	Volume	Baker's %
Unsalted butter	330 g	11.64 oz	1½ cups	47.8

Procedure:

Two days before baking:

1. Bring the eggs and milk to 60 to 65°F (16 to 18°C). Place all the dough ingredients (milk first to prevent sticking) in the bowl of a 5-quart (5 L) stand mixer and use a dough hook to mix at low speed until the dough comes together. This process should take 3 to 4 minutes.

2. Increase the mixer speed to medium and continue to mix for an additional minute.

3. Remove the dough from the mixer and place in a proofing container sprayed with nonstick cooking spray. Check the dough temperature (ideal would be 75° to 78°F (24° to 26°C). Cover the dough with plastic wrap and let bulk ferment at room temperature for about 2 hours.

The FRIDGE and the FREEZER FLIP-FLOP

You may ask yourself, what is the point of the seemingly constant back and forth between the refrigerator and freezer and working with the dough? The constant jockeying of temperatures does serve a purpose.

When laminating dough, it is important to keep the consistency of the butter block and the dough essentially the same. If the butter is too soft, it could be squeezed out during the process, but if it is too hard, it can crack and break through the dough.

When you remove both the dough and butter block from the refrigerator, you will notice that the butter is harder—which is why it goes through the softening process to make it pliable. But when you start the rolling process of lamination, the surface of the dough starts to warm up and it changes consistency, too.

The frequent set changes between the refrigerator and the freezer maintain the delicate balance between the two components, thereby ensuring a perfectly laminated dough in the end.

---

4. After 2 hours of bulk fermentation, loosely shape the dough into a rectangle and place on a parchment-lined half sheet pan. Cover with plastic wrap and refrigerate overnight. Scale out the butter and make the butter block (see page 133) and refrigerate overnight.

Day before baking:

1. Remove the dough from the refrigerator and place in the freezer for about 30 minutes. While the dough is in the freezer, remove the butter block from the refrigerator and soften by hammering it with a rolling pin to a pliable consistency (see page 60).

2. Remove the dough from the freezer and roll out to a 16 x 8-inch (40.6 x 20.3 cm) rectangle.

Place the butter block in the center of the dough (short sides of butter touching long sides of dough) and fold the short edges of the dough toward each other to meet in the center. Press the edges together with your hands.

3. Follow the steps described on page 134 to laminate the dough, performing a total of 3 trifolds to yield 27 layers.

4. Place the dough onto a parchment-lined sheet pan and cover with plastic wrap. Put the dough into the freezer for 1 hour to rest, then remove and put into the refrigerator overnight.

Continued on page 138

All-Purpose Danish (continued)

Baking day:

1. Remove the dough from the refrigerator and place in the freezer for about 30 minutes.

2. Remove from the freezer and roll out the dough until it is about ¼ inch (6 mm) thick.

3. Now comes the fun part—deciding how you would like to embellish your Danish creations! A skim through chapter 7 will reveal a variety of fillings and toppings, from sweet pastry cream and lemon curd to savory spreads. Some can be baked along with the dough and others are added after the oven. Here are a few shapes and combinations to inspire:

4. Preheat a convection oven to 350°C (180°C, gas mark 4) for about 30 minutes before baking.

5. Bake on a parchment-lined sheet pan in the preheated convection oven for 15 to 18 minutes, depending on the shapes and fillings.

Flower: fold square in half, make two short straight cuts and one right-angle cut; fold in outer corners

Wrap: fold in two corners together

Pocket: fold in four corners together

Palette: fold square in half; make one long cut, open, and fold back outer edge onto itself

Pinwheel: make 4 cuts on the diagonal, fold the top left corner of each triangle into the center.

SWEET OPTIONS

Some sweet Danish creations with pastry cream (a), fruit (b), chocolate (c), and nut filling

SAVORY OPTIONS

Savory version of dough scraps mixed with pesto and cheese (d), and another with tomato sauce, cheese, and sesame seeds (e) and pesto-cheese coating (f).

Piping pastry cream into the center

Coating dough with pesto sauce

Pastry cream with apricots, ready-to-bake

Savory appetizers with tomato sauce, cheese, seeds, and spices

Ready-to-bake Danish with nut filling and chocolate

Pesto tartlets, ready-to-bake

Croissants ● DVD CONTENT

YIELD:	**about 12 croissants**
BAKING TEMPERATURE:	**360°F (182°C, gas mark 4)**
BAKING TIME:	**12 to 15 minutes**
TOTAL TIME:	**32 hours over 3 days (1 hour total of active work)**

The croissant—the French delight, baked to perfection. Yes, they really do eat croissants for breakfast in France, and yes, one bite will transport you to the tiny courtyard of a Left Bank boutique hotel. In one word: heavenly. Even though a traditional croissant dough is lean—meaning the dough does not include any fat (such as milk, eggs, or butter), I have had great success in using the All-Purpose Danish dough for making croissants. The croissant (pronounced *krwuh-SAHN*, in French—if you are going to take the time to make these by hand, then you must learn to pronounce them, too!) is to breakfast pastry as the baguette is to artisan bread. So, while you might not be able to judge a book by its cover, you can definitely judge a baker by their baguette and croissant. That might be intimidating, but don't let it stop you! After all, you never know where a homemade croissant and butter will take you.

Ingredient	Metric	Weight	Volume
All-Purpose Danish dough (page 136) (including its butter block, page 133)	1 batch	1 batch	1 batch
Egg Wash (page 152)	1 batch	1 batch	1 batch

Procedure:

  Two days before baking:

  Follow directions for Danish dough: mix the dough, allow to bulk ferment, shape into a loose rectangle, cover, and place in the refrigerator overnight. Prepare the butter block and place in refrigerator overnight.

  Day before baking:

  Follow directions for the Danish dough: remove the dough and butter from the refrigerator, place the dough in the freezer for 30 minutes, make the butter block pliable, laminate the dough to 27 layers, cover with plastic wrap and place in the freezer for 1 hour, then remove and place in the refrigerator overnight.

Baking day:

1. Remove the dough from the refrigerator and place in the freezer for about 30 minutes. Remove from the freezer and on a lightly floured surface, roll out the dough lengthwise to ¼ inch (6 mm) thick. This process is strenuous and you may need to return the dough to the freezer and let it rest for 10 minutes between passes. The dough should reach a final size of approximately 11 x 18 inches (27.9 x 45.7 cm). Use a pastry wheel to trim all edges straight and square.

2. Using a ruler, measure and mark 3-inch (7.6 cm) intervals along the entire length of both long sides of the dough. Again, use a ruler to connect the corresponding marks opposite each other and lightly score the dough with a pastry wheel. Do not cut through the dough **(a)**.

3. Choose one edge, and for each strip, mark the center of the strip in the dough on this edge. Now take the ruler and connect the center point to the ends of the strip opposite it, creating long triangles of dough.

4. To shape the croissants, place a long triangle in front of you on the table (tip toward you). Start with the base of the triangle and roll the dough up completely **(b)**.

5. Place the croissants, seam side down, on a parchment-lined sheet pan. Cover with plastic wrap and let proof at room temperature for 2½ to 3 hours.

The Shape of CROISSANTS

Many people think croissants are traditionally shaped with a bend, and they might be right, depending on the type of fat used. In France, croissants that are made with any amount of shortening will be shaped in a curved crescent shape. Those that are made with butter are straight, making it easy to identify the difference in the display case. Feel free to curve your croissants if you like, but since these are made with pure butter, I respect the French tradition and always roll them straight.

6. Preheat a convection oven to 360°F (182°C, gas mark 4) about 30 minutes before baking.

7. Just before baking, brush the croissants with egg wash in the direction of the roll **(c)**. Bake in the preheated convection oven for 12 to 15 minutes. The croissants are done baking when a nice golden brown develops on the crust.

8. Remove the croissants from the sheet pan after baking and allow to cool on a wire rack. Enjoy while warm or at room temperature. These do not store well and are best consumed within a day of baking.

a) **Measure and mark** intervals with a ruler and then cut the long triangles of dough.

b) **Roll up the croissants,** starting with the base of the triangle.

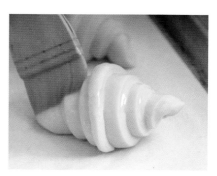

c) **Brush the tops** of the croissants with egg wash just before baking.

Whole Wheat Ham and Cheese Croissants

YIELD:	**16 croissants**
BAKING TEMPERATURE:	**360°F (182°C, gas mark 4) convection mode**
BAKING TIME:	**15 to 18 minutes**
TOTAL TIME:	**32 hours over 3 days (1 hour total of active work)**

This whole wheat version of laminated dough adds a touch of health into the world of breakfast pastries. It pairs nicely with savory flavors, but you can substitute this dough in any of the previous Danish variations as well. Try it with the ham and cheese croissant version that follows and turn any scraps into an easy savory monkey bread. Or make it plain and sweeten it up with a sugar glaze—its versatility is the key.

Procedure:

Two days before baking:

1. Bring the eggs and milk to 60 to 65°F (16 to 18°C). Place the milk, flours, egg yolk, salt, sugar, yeast, and butter in the bowl of a 5-quart (5 L) stand mixer and use a dough hook to mix at low speed until the dough comes together. This should take 2 to 4 minutes.

2. Increase the mixer speed to medium and continue to mix for an additional minute.

3. Remove the dough from the mixer and place in a proofing container sprayed with nonstick cooking spray. Check the dough temperature (ideal would be 75° to 78°F (24° to 26°C). Cover the dough with plastic wrap and let bulk ferment at room temperature for about 2 hours.

4. After 2 hours of bulk fermentation, loosely shape the dough into a rectangle and place on a parchment-lined sheet pan. Cover with plastic wrap and refrigerate overnight. Scale out the butter and make the butter block (see page 133) and refrigerate overnight.

Dough

Ingredient	Metric	Weight	Volume	Baker's %
Whole milk	240 g	8.46 oz	1 cup	48
Bread flour	375 g	13.22 oz	3 cups	75
Whole wheat flour	125 g	4.4 oz	1 cup	25
Egg yolk	75 g	2.64 oz	3 yolks	15
Salt	10 g	0.35 oz	1½ tsp	2
Granulated sugar	50 g	1.76 oz	¼ cup	10
Instant yeast, preferably osmotolerant	8 g	0.28 oz	2 tsp	1.6
Unsalted butter	28 g	0.98 oz	2 tbsp	5.6
Ham (optional)	150 g	5.3 oz	4–1.25 oz slices	n/a
Cheese (optional)	225 g	8 oz	8–1 oz slices	n/a
Egg Wash (page 152)	1 batch	1 batch	1 batch	n/a
Sesame seeds (optional)	As needed	As needed	As needed	As needed

Butter Block

Ingredient	Metric	Weight	Volume	Baker's %
Unsalted butter, 83% butterfat	224 g	7.9 oz	1 cup	44.8

Day before baking:

1. Remove the dough from the refrigerator and place in the freezer for about 30 minutes. While the dough is in the freezer, remove the butter block from the refrigerator and soften by hammering it with a rolling pin to a pliable consistency (see page 60).

2. Remove the dough from the freezer and roll out to a 16 x 8-inch (40.6 x 20.3 cm) rectangle. Place the butter block in the center of the dough (short sides of butter touching long sides of dough) and fold the short edges of the dough toward each other to meet in the center. Press the edges together with you hands.

3. Follow the steps described on page 134 to laminate the dough, giving 2 trifolds right away. Place the dough in the freezer for 30 minutes, then remove to give the last trifold.

4. Place the dough on a parchment-lined sheet pan and cover with plastic wrap. Put the dough into the freezer for 1 hour to rest, then remove and put into the refrigerator overnight.

Baking day:

1. Cut the ham and cheese into strips (about 3 x ½ inch [7.6 x 1.3 cm]) and set aside.

2. Remove the dough from the refrigerator and place in the freezer for about 30 minutes. Remove from the freezer and on a lightly floured surface, roll the dough out lengthwise to ¼ inch (6 mm) thick. This process is strenuous and you may need to return the dough to the freezer and let it rest for 10 minutes between passes. The dough should reach a final size of approximately 11 x 18 inches (27.9 x 45.7 cm). Use a pastry wheel to trim all edges straight and square.

3. Using a ruler, measure and mark 3-inch (7.6 cm) intervals along the entire length of both long sides of the dough. Again, use a ruler to connect the corresponding marks opposite each other and lightly score the dough with a pastry wheel (do not cut through the dough.)

4. Choose one edge, and for each strip, mark the center of the strip in the dough on this edge. Now take the ruler and connect the center point to the ends of the strip opposite it, creating long triangles of dough.

5. To shape the croissants, place a long triangle in front of you on the table (tip toward you). Lay a strip of ham and cheese close to the base of the triangle. Start with the base of the triangle and roll the dough up completely **(a, b)**.

6. Place the croissants, seam side down, on a parchment-lined sheet pan. Cover with plastic wrap and let proof at room temperature for 2½ to 3 hours.

7. Preheat the convection oven to 360°F (182°C, gas mark 4) about 30 minutes before baking.

8. Just before baking, brush the croissants with egg wash in the direction of the roll (see page 141.) Sprinkle with sesame seeds if desired **(c)**. Bake in the preheated convection oven for 15 to 18 minutes. The croissants are done baking when a nice golden brown develops on the crust.

9. Remove the croissants from the sheet pan after baking and allow to cool on a wire rack. Enjoy while warm or at room temperature. These do not store well and are best consumed within a day of baking.

a) **Lay the ham and cheese** near the base of the triangle and roll up the dough.

b) **Roll up** the dough.

c) **Brush the tops** with egg wash and sprinkle with some sesame seeds if desired.

Ultimate Chocolate Croissants

YIELD:	**12 to 14 croissants**
BAKING TEMPERATURE:	**360°F (182°C, gas mark 4) convection mode**
BAKING TIME:	**12 to 15 minutes**
TOTAL TIME:	**32 hours over 3 days (1 hour total of active work)**

Flaky chocolatey layers of dough wrapped around a stick of chocolate, baked to perfection—what could be better? This recipe uses cardamom, a warm spice that is a member of the ginger family and is one of the most expensive spices by weight. Luckily its intense aromatic qualities mean that a little goes a long way. Many pastry chefs and artisan chocolatiers artfully pair this alluring spice with chocolate to create a symphony of flavors.

Procedure:

Two days before baking:

1. Bring the eggs and milk to 60 to 65°F (16 to 18°C). Place all the dough ingredients (milk first to prevent sticking) through the 14 g of butter in the bowl of a 5-quart (5 L) stand mixer and use a dough hook to mix at low speed until the dough comes together.

2. Increase the mixer speed to medium and continue to mix for an additional minute.

3. Remove the dough from the mixer and place in a proofing container sprayed with nonstick cooking spray **(a)**. Check the dough temperature (ideal would be 75° to 78°F (24° to 26°C). Cover the dough with plastic wrap and let bulk ferment at room temperature for about 2 hours.

4. After 2 hours of bulk fermentation, loosely shape the dough into a rectangle and place on a parchment-lined sheet pan. Cover with plastic wrap and refrigerate overnight. Scale out the butter and make the butter block (see page 133) and refrigerate overnight

Dough

Ingredient	Metric	Weight	Volume	Baker's %
Whole milk	265 g	9.34 oz	1⅛ cups	50
Bread flour	530 g	18.69 oz	4 cups	100
Unsweetened cocoa powder	25 g	0.88 oz	¼ cup	4.7 oz
Egg, whole	50 g	1.76 oz	1 egg	9.4
Egg yolks	34 g	1.19 oz	2 yolks	6.4
Granulated sugar	65 g	2.29 oz	½ cup	12.2
Salt	10 g	0.35 oz	1½ tsp	1.8 oz
Instant yeast	6 g	0.21 oz	1½ tsp	1.1
Ground cardamom	1 g	0.03 oz	1½ tsp	0.1
Unsalted butter	14 g	0.49 oz	1 tbsp	2.6
Nut Filling (optional, page 154)	1 batch	1 batch	1 batch	n/a
Chocolate baking sticks (batons) or chocolate chips	About 16	About 16	About 16	n/a
Cinnamon Sugar (optional, page 151)	As desired	As desired	As desired	n/a

Butter Block

Ingredient	Metric	Weight	Volume	Baker's %
Unsalted butter, 83% butterfat	225 g	7.93 oz	1 cup	42.4

Day before baking:

1. Remove the dough from the refrigerator and place in the freezer for about 30 minutes. While the dough is in the freezer, remove the butter block from the refrigerator and soften by hammering it with a rolling pin to a pliable consistency (see page 60).

2. Remove the dough from the freezer and roll out to a 16 x 8-inch (40.6 x 45.7 cm) rectangle. Place the butter block in the center of the dough (short sides of butter touching long sides of dough) and fold the short edges of the dough toward each other to meet in the center. Press the edges together with your hands.

3. Follow the steps described on page 134 to laminate the dough, giving 2 trifolds right away. Place the dough into the freezer for 30 minutes, then remove to give the last trifold.

4. Place the dough on a parchment-lined sheet pan and cover with plastic wrap. Put the dough into the freezer for 1 hour to rest, then remove and put into the refrigerator overnight.

Baking day:

1. Make a batch of Nut Filling (this can also be made the day before).

2. Remove the dough from the refrigerator and place into the freezer for about 30 minutes. Remove from the freezer and on a lightly floured surface, roll the dough out lengthwise to ¼ inch (6 mm) thick. This process is strenuous and you may need to return the dough to the freezer and let it rest for 10 minutes between passes. The dough should reach a final size of approximately 11 x 18 inches (27.9 x 45.7 cm). Use a pastry wheel to trim all edges straight and square.

3. Using a ruler, measure and mark 3-inch (7.6 cm) intervals along the entire length of both long sides of the dough. Again, use a ruler to connect the corresponding marks opposite each other and lightly score the dough with a pastry wheel (do not cut through the dough.)

4. Choose one edge, and for each strip, mark the center of the strip in the dough on this edge. Now take the ruler and connect the center point to the ends of the strip opposite it, creating long triangles of dough.

5. To shape the croissants, place a long triangle in front of you on the table (tip toward you). About an inch away from the base, place about a tablespoon of Nut Filling on the dough and lay a chocolate baking stick onto the paste. The ends of the chocolate will go beyond the edges of the dough. Start with the base of the triangle and roll up the dough completely **(b)**.

6. Place the croissants, seam side down, on a parchment-lined sheet pan. Cover with plastic wrap and let proof at room temperature for 2½ to 3 hours.

7. Preheat a convection oven to 360°F (182°C, gas mark 4) about 30 minutes before baking.

8. Just before baking, spritz the tops of the croissants with some water and sprinkle on a bit of cinnamon sugar if desired. Bake in the preheated convection oven for 12 to 15 minutes. It is a bit difficult to tell if the croissants are done by looking at the color since they are already dark before baking **(c)**.

9. Remove the croissants from the sheet pan after baking and allow to cool on a wire rack. Enjoy while warm or at room temperature. These do not store well and are best consumed within a day of baking.

a) **The dough as it looks** when it comes off the mixer.

b) **Roll the chocolate stick** into the croissant.

c) **Just before baking,** spritz with water and sprinkle on cinnamon sugar if desired.

Chocolate-Cinnamon Swirls

YIELD:	**10 to 12 buns**
BAKING TEMPERATURE:	**350°F (180°C, gas mark 4) convection mode**
BAKING TIME:	**15 to 20 minutes**
TOTAL TIME:	**32 hours over 3 days (1 hour total of active work)**

Once you have taken the time to make the chocolate laminated dough for the Ultimate Chocolate Croissant, why not make a few Chocolate Cinnamon Swirls while you are at it? Doubling the recipe is not possible (it's highly unlikely you have a 10-quart [10 L] mixer at home), but using half for croissants and half for cinnamon buns works just fine! Or mix up an entire batch of dough just for the buns alone—whatever your fancy. This version builds upon the main dough formula from the chocolate croissant and takes it in another direction.

Dough

Ingredient	Metric	Weight	Volume	Baker's %
Ultimate Chocolate Croissant dough (page 144, including its butter block)	1 batch	1 batch	1 batch	n/a
Cinnamon Sugar (page 151)	As needed	As needed	As needed	n/a

Procedure:

Two days before baking:

1. Follow directions for Ultimate Chocolate Croissant dough: mix up a batch of dough, allow it to bulk ferment, cover with plastic wrap, and place it in the refrigerator overnight. Make the butter block and refrigerate overnight.

Day before baking:

1. Follow directions for Ultimate Chocolate Croissants: Remove the dough from the refrigerator and freeze for about 30 minutes. Soften the butter block into a pliable consistency. Remove the dough from the freezer and follow the steps to roll out and laminate. Freeze the laminated dough for 1 hour, then refrigerate overnight.

Not Just for CHOCOLATE LOVERS

If you prefer to use the all-purpose Danish or the whole wheat Danish dough for this recipe, go right ahead! Any laminated dough works well with the Cinnamon Sugar mix. Enjoy!

Baking day:

1. Prepare a batch of Cinnamon Sugar.

2. Remove the dough from the refrigerator and place in the freezer for about 30 minutes. Remove from the freezer and on a lightly floured surface, roll the dough out lengthwise to ¼ inch (6 mm) thick. This process is strenuous and you may need to return the dough to the freezer and let it rest for 10 minutes between passes. The dough should reach a final size of approximately 11 x 18 inches (28 x 46 cm). Use a pastry wheel to trim all edges straight and square.

3. Spray the entire surface of dough and spread out the Cinnamon Sugar evenly, leaving a 1-inch (2.5 cm) buffer of plain dough along one long side.

4. Start with the long side that has the filling and roll up the dough like a jelly roll. If you want your final roll to bake with a soft, even contour, then gently and loosely roll the dough. If you want a roll with a bit more expansive character, then roll up the dough a bit more firmly **(a)**.

5. Prepare standard muffin tins with nonstick cooking spray. Use a sharp knife to slice the log into 1½-inch (3.8 cm) sections and place in the muffin tins **(b)**.

6. Cover with plastic wrap and allow to proof for 2 to 2½ hours at room temperature **(c)**.

7. Preheat the convection oven to 350°F (180°C, gas mark 4) about 30 minutes before baking.

8. Bake in the preheated convection oven for 15 to 20 minutes.

9. Immediately remove the rolls from the muffin tins and toss lightly in a bowl of cinnamon sugar until they are completely coated. Place on a cool tray and let cool before eating **(d)**.

a) **Spread out** the cinnamon sugar and roll up the dough.

b) **Slice the log** into 1½-inch (3.8 cm) sections and place in muffin tins.

c) **The swirls** are proofed and ready to bake.

d) **Toss in cinnamon sugar** while still hot from the oven.

CHAPTER SEVEN

Fillings, Glazes, Toppings, and Spreads

WHENEVER I WALK INTO A BAKERY OR PASTRY SHOP and see the glass vitrines filled with tempting delights, my willpower melts away. The seductive shine of a sugar glaze hypnotizes and the nutty toppings just beg to be tasted. How can anyone resist?

I have determined that much of the credit for these enticements often goes to the final touches. There appears to be something in the way a croissant can be egg washed just right so the light catches the shine as the golden caramel color radiates through to the surface. Or how the rich sunshine yellow of a pastry cream nestles into the center of a warm Danish, hinting at the smooth creamy texture waiting to be savored with the crisp, flaky layers of dough.

This chapter is literally the icing on the cake, and then some. The following recipes are intended to be used in combination with others in the book; sometimes they play a starring role and other times they simply enhance and support the flavors already present. What I find so appealing about these extras is that they can often be substituted for one another, depending on your mood and tastes. Or better yet, start to experiment and create your own using the foundation formulas and substituting other ingredients and flavors. An easy way to start is by a simple change in extracts. There are so many different extracts and compounds just waiting to contribute a burst of new flavor. And while this book is focused on the sweeter side of the day, there are savory applications, too. Included are some great spreads to be enjoyed on bagels and other brunch-type breads that will add a bit of spice to your life if your sweet tooth has been satisfied. In general, it is my hope that all of these formulas add to the enjoyment of the fruits of your labor —*bon appétit!*

Almond Bostock Paste

A nutty spread to bake with Bostock (page 118) or as a Danish filling variation (page 136). Makes about 1 cup (192 g).

Ingredient	Metric	Weight	Volume
Unsalted butter	42 g	1.48 oz	3 tbsp
Eggs, whole	50 g	1.76 oz	1 egg
Granulated sugar	50 g	1.76 oz	¼ cup
Almond or hazelnut flour	50 g	1.76 oz	½ cup
Orange zest	¼ orange	¼ orange	¼ orange

Bring the butter and eggs to room temperature. Cream the butter and granulated sugar together. Whisk the egg before slowly creaming it in stages into the butter mixture. Add the almond flour and orange zest and mix into a smooth consistency. Place in a container, cover, and refrigerate overnight.

Almond Paste Filling

An almond filling that bakes up with a light, airy texture. Makes about ¾ cup (380 g).

Ingredient	Metric	Weight	Volume
Almond paste	350 g	12.34 oz	⅔ cup
Lemon zest	½ lemon	½ lemon	½ lemon
Egg whites	30 g	1 oz	1 egg white

In the bowl of a 5-quart (5 L) stand mixer, soften the almond paste by mixing it at low speed with a paddle attachment. Add the lemon zest and mix it in. Slowly add the egg whites and mix until a soft consistency is achieved. You may not need to add all of the whites. The filling should be able to be rolled out into logs without having to add any flour to prevent sticking.

Bostock Syrup

A sweet orange syrup for Bostock (page 118), but can be brushed on the tops of most anything for a quick blast of flavor. Makes about 1⅓ cups (300 g).

Ingredient	Metric	Weight	Volume
Water	100 g	3.52 oz	½ cup
Granulated sugar	100 g	3.52 oz	½ cup
Light corn syrup	100 g	3.52 oz	⅓ cup
Orange	1 medium orange	1 medium orange	1 medium orange

Combine the water, granulated sugar, and corn syrup in a saucepan and bring to a boil over medium-high heat. Remove from the heat. Slice the orange into ¼-inch (6 mm) slices and add them to the warm syrup. Cover and let cool to room temperature, then place in the refrigerator to soak overnight.

Butterkuchen Paste

Be warned: This almond flavored paste is quite addictive. Use it in the Apple Kuchen (page 108) or simply spread it on your favorite bread. Makes about ½ cup (165 g).

Ingredient	Metric	Weight	Volume
Almond paste	165 g	5.82 oz	⅓ cup
Lemon zest	⅓ lemon	⅓ lemon	⅓ lemon
Unsweetened butter, softened	As needed	As needed	As needed

In the bowl of a 5-quart (5 L) stand mixer, cream together the almond paste and lemon zest. Slowly add the (room temperature) softened butter and cream until you attain a frosting-like consistency that can be piped in a pastry bag. Use the Butterkuchen Paste immediately; otherwise, place in a plastic container, cover, and refrigerate overnight.

Chocolate Glaze

This glaze is great to use with any brioche recipe. Simply spread evenly on the top just before baking and the brioche (or other creation) will have a slightly crunchy chocolate texture. Makes about 2 cups (372 g).

Ingredient	Metric	Weight	Volume
Granulated sugar	165 g	5.82 oz	¾ cup
Almond flour	82 g	2.89 oz	¾ cup
Vegetable oil	13 g	0.45 oz	1 tbsp
Cornstarch	7 g	0.24 oz	1 tbsp
Unsweetened cocoa powder	7 g	0.24 oz	2 tbsp
Vanilla extract	16 g	0.56 oz	4 tbsp
Egg whites	82 g	2.3 oz	3 egg whites

Place all the ingredients in a mixing bowl and stir together with a spatula until smooth. If the glaze seems too thick, you can thin it down with some additional egg whites. Apply to the tops of brioche with a spoon or piping bag just before baking. For a crackled effect, dust heavily with powdered sugar before baking. Another nice variation is to sprinkle chopped almond slivers on top of the glaze.

Cinnamon Bun Filling

A sandlike cinnamon sugar spread that makes a cinnamon bun what it is! Makes about ⅔ cup (161 g).

Ingredient	Metric	Weight	Volume
Unsalted butter, softened	20 g	0.70 oz	1½ tbsp
Light brown sugar	120 g	4.23 oz	½ cup
Ground cinnamon	11 g	0.38 oz	4 tsp
Bread or all-purpose flour	10 g	0.35 oz	1 tbsp

Bring the butter to room temperature and cream together with the light brown sugar. Add the ground cinnamon and flour and blend together, scraping the bottom of the bowl periodically. The consistency will be very crumbly, almost sandlike. Store in a plastic food storage bag for up to 1 week in the refrigerator.

Cinnamon Sugar

The name says it all—a great balance of sugar and cinnamon for many uses. Makes about 1 cup (204 g).

Ingredient	Metric	Weight	Volume
Granulated sugar	200 g	7.05 oz	1 cup
Ground cinnamon	4 g	0.14 oz	2 tsp

Add the ground cinnamon to the granulated sugar and stir together with a whisk. Store in an airtight container for up to 4 months at room temperature.

Crumb Topping DVD CONTENT

A versatile crumb topping—perfect on top of muffins, quick breads, and more! Makes about 2⅓ cups (398 g).

Ingredient	Metric	Weight	Volume
Bread or all-purpose flour	160 g	5.64 oz	1⅓ cup
Light brown sugar	120 g	4.23 oz	½ cup
Ground cinnamon	1.5 g	0.05 oz	¾ tsp
Salt	0.6 g	0.02 oz	⅛ tsp
Unsalted butter	115 g	4 oz	½ cup
Baking powder	0.6 g	0.02 oz	⅛ tsp

Combine all the ingredients in the mixing bowl of a 5-quart (5 L) stand mixer, and use a paddle attachment to blend together until the desired texture is achieved. Take care not to overmix. This can also be done by hand using a pastry cutter or by using two sharp knives, finishing with your hands.

Crunch Topping DVD CONTENT

A nuttier version of crumb topping—adds crunch and texture! Makes about 1½ cups (250 g).

Ingredient	Metric	Weight	Volume
Pecans	55 g	2 oz	½ cup
Rolled oats	34 g	1.19 oz	¼ cup
Unsalted butter	56 g	2 oz	4 tbsp
All-purpose flour	57 g	2 oz	½ cup
Granulated sugar	45 g	1.58 oz	¼ cup
Ground cinnamon	1 g	0.03 oz	½ tsp
Salt	0.5 g	0.01 oz	⅛ tsp
Baking powder	0.5 g	0.01 oz	⅛ tsp
Orange zest	½ orange	½ orange	½ orange

Chop the pecans and oats to a coarse chop, either by hand or in a food processor. Melt the butter and allow it to cool. Combine all the ingredients together in a bowl and mix until a lumpy consistency is achieved. Store in an airtight container for up to 1 week in the refrigerator.

Egg Wash

Everyone needs a simple egg wash to count on—this is mine. Makes about ½ cup (125 g).

Ingredient	Metric	Weight	Volume
Eggs, whole	100 g	3.52 oz	2 eggs
Egg yolks	25 g	0.88 oz	1 yolk
Salt	Pinch	Pinch	Pinch

Whisk the eggs and yolk together along with the salt until well blended. Cover and refrigerate and use within 1 day.

Lemon-Almond Glaze

A tangy citrus alternative to the Chocolate Glaze. Makes about 1¾ cups (275 g).

Ingredient	Metric	Weight	Volume
Granulated sugar	130 g	4.58 oz	⅔ cup
Almond flour or meal	60 g	2.11 oz	⅔ cup
Vegetable oil	10 g	0.35 oz	2 tbsp
Cornstarch	5 g	0.17 oz	2 tsp
Vanilla extract	10 g	0.35 oz	2½ tsp
Lemon zest	¼ lemon	¼ lemon	¼ lemon
Egg whites	About 60 g	2.11 oz	About 3 egg whites

Place all the ingredients except the egg whites in a mixing bowl and stir together until well blended. Slowly add the egg whites and stir until a smooth consistency is achieved (it should be similar to a thick honey). If the glaze is too thick, thin it by adding additional egg whites. Cover with a sheet of plastic wrap and store in the refrigerator for up to 2 days.

Lemon Cream

Light and creamy and lemony, it's just the right touch for brioche. Makes about 1 cup (262 g).

Ingredient	Metric	Weight	Volume
Heavy cream	150 g	5.29 oz	⅔ cup
Granulated sugar	12 g	0.24 oz	1 tbsp
Lemon curd	100 g	3.52	⅓ cup

Using a 5-quart (5 L) stand mixer with a whisk attachment or electric hand beaters, whip the heavy cream and granulated sugar together to soft peaks. In a separate bowl, whisk the lemon curd by hand to a smooth consistency. Gently fold the lemon curd into the whipped cream in stages until combined. Use immediately.

Lemon Curd

Another stand-by favorite that you will turn to again and again. Makes about 1¼ cups (390 g).

Ingredient	Metric	Weight	Volume
Egg yolks	120 g	4.23 oz	6 yolks
Granulated sugar	100 g	3.52 oz	½ cup
Lemon juice, fresh	112 g	3.95 oz	½ cup (about 3 large lemons)
Lemon zest	1 g	0.03 oz	½ lemon
Unsalted butter, cut into small cubes	56 g	1.97 oz	4 tbsp

Line the bottom of a rimmed sheet pan or shallow baking pan with a layer of plastic wrap. Place all ingredients in a heavy-bottomed saucepan. Cook over medium-high heat, stirring constantly with a whisk, paying careful attention not to burn. As the curd thickens, reduce the heat and continue stirring. Once the curd starts to bubble, remove the pan from the heat. Scrape the lemon curd out of the saucepan and onto the plastic-lined pan. Use a spatula to spread evenly in the pan (to between ½ and 1 inch [1.3 and 2.5 cm] thick). (Note: it is not necessary for the curd to cover the entire bottom of the pan.) Cover the top of the lemon curd with another sheet of plastic wrap and refrigerate up to 2 days.

Lemon-Sugar Glaze

A refreshing citrus glaze, especially nice on muffins and quick breads. Makes about 1½ cups (340 g).

Ingredient	Metric	Weight	Volume
Confectioners' sugar	270 g	9.5 oz	2⅔ cups
Fresh lemon juice	70 g	2.4 oz	2 fluid oz (12 tbsp)

Using a whisk, combine the confectioners' sugar with the lemon juice until a smooth consistency is reached.

Honey-Nut Butter

Sweet and nutty—makes the morning brioche, or even toast, come to life. Makes about ¾ cup (188 g).

Ingredient	Metric	Weight	Volume
Walnuts or pecans	25 g	0.88 oz	⅓ cup
Unsalted butter	125 g	4.4 oz	9 tbsp
Honey	38 g	1.34 oz	2 tbsp

Toast the nuts on a sheet pan for 7 to 10 minutes at 400°F (200°C, gas mark 6), shaking the pan halfway through the toasting process. Remove from the oven and let cool before chopping. In a mixing bowl, blend together by hand the softened butter and honey, until smooth and creamy. Add the toasted and chopped pecans and blend until evenly distributed.

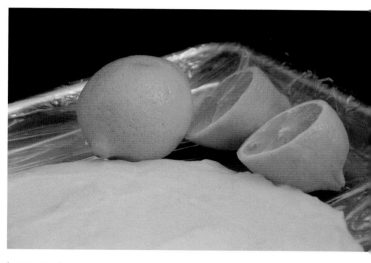

Lemon curd

Nut Filling

A moist and sweet filling that adds a delicate nut flavor to a variety of baked goods. Makes about 1¾ cups (310 g).

Ingredient	Metric	Weight	Volume
Nut flour*	125 g	4.4 oz	1¼ cup
Granulated sugar	100 g	3.52 oz	½ cup
Corn syrup	25 g	0.88 oz	1½ tbsp
Lemon zest	⅛ lemon, only if making pistachio paste	⅛ lemon, only if making pistachio paste	⅛ lemon, only if making pistachio paste
Lemon zest	1 g, only if making pistachio paste	0.03 oz, only if making pistachio paste	½ tsp, only if making pistachio paste
Water	Up to 60 g	2.11 oz	Up to 6 tbsp

*Use almond, hazelnut, or pistachio nuts.

Combine all of the ingredients except the water and blend together by hand (if using hazelnuts, you can also add ¼ teaspoon [0.5 g] of ground cinnamon). Slowly add the water to achieve a nice spreadable consistency (it should not tear the dough when it is spread.) Place in a plastic container with a cover and store in the refrigerator for up to a week. The consistency can be adjusted with water on the day of use.

Note: Pistachio flour tends to require less water; when making a pistachio nut filling, start with half the water and adjust to the desired consistency.

Pastry Cream

An indispensable formula that all bakers need in their repertoire! Makes about 1½ cups (400 g).

Ingredient	Metric	Weight	Volume
Whole milk	250 g	8.81 oz	1 cup
Vanilla extract	4 g	0.14 oz	1 tsp
Vanilla bean (optional)	¼ bean	¼ bean	¼ bean
Granulated sugar	60 g	2.11 oz	4 tbsp
Egg yolks	50 g	1.76 oz	3 yolks
Cornstarch	20 g	0.70 oz	2 tbsp
Unsalted butter	14 g	0.49 oz	1 tbsp

In a saucepan, bring the milk, vanilla extract, vanilla bean, and half of the sugar to a boil, stirring constantly as it starts to boil. While the milk is first heating, combine the egg yolk along with the cornstarch and second half of sugar in a separate bowl and whisk until a smooth consistency is achieved. After the milk mixture boils, temper the eggs by slowly adding some of the hot milk mixture to the egg mixture, whisking constantly (remove the vanilla bean if necessary). Keep whisking and add about half of the milk mixture. Now start to pour this mixture back into the hot milk, whisking constantly over low heat. The cream will start to thicken—make sure you keep stirring, not just in the center, but the bottom and sides as well. As soon as the cream starts to bubble, remove it from the heat and stir in the butter. Line a rimmed sheet pan with plastic wrap and pour the pastry cream into the sheet pan. Cover the top of the cream with plastic wrap so that it touches the cream, sealing out any air. Place in the refrigerator to chill and store up to 1 day. Before using, gently mix the cream with a spatula or whisk.

Pastry cream (page 154)

Pumpkin Pastry Cream

Delicious in the Pumpkin Cream Brioche (page 104), but is a nice sweet filling for whenever you need one Makes about 2 cups (595 g).

Ingredient	Metric	Weight	Volume
Whole milk	330 g	11.64 oz	1½ cup
Granulated sugar	66 g	2.32 oz	4 tbsp
Egg yolks	60 g	2.11 oz	3 yolks
Ground cinnamon	0.6 g	0.02 oz	¼ tsp
Ground nutmeg	0.3 g	0.01 oz	⅛ tsp
Ground cloves	0.3 g	0.01 oz	⅛ tsp
Ground ginger	0.3 g	0.01 oz	⅛ tsp
Cornstarch	25 g	0.88 oz	3 tbsp
Pumpkin puree	83 g	2.92 oz	⅓ cup
Honey	25 g	0.88 oz	1½ tbsp
Vanilla extract	5 g	0.17 oz	½ tbsp
Vanilla bean, split	⅓ bean	⅓ bean	⅓ bean
Unsalted butter	28 g	1 oz	3 tbsp

Follow the same procedure for the basic pastry cream, adding the spices along with the cornstarch to the egg yolks and second portion of sugar. After this has been mixed, add the pumpkin puree to the egg mixture and combine. Continue with the basic pastry cream formula by tempering the hot milk into the pumpkin egg mixture and follow the remainder of the directions.

Sautéed Apples

Not only for the Apple Kuchen formula (page 108)—use them as a Danish filling, too. Makes about 1 cup (500 g).

Ingredient	Metric	Weight	Volume
Firm, tart apples (e.g., Fuji or Granny Smith)	4 medium apples	4 medium apples	4 medium apples
Vanilla bean or extract	1 bean or 10 g extract	1 bean or 1½ tsp extract	1 bean or 1½ tsp extract
Unsalted butter	42 g	1.48 oz	3 tbsp
Light brown sugar	45 g	1.58 oz	¼ cup, packed
Lemon zest	1 lemon	1 lemon	1 lemon

Peel and core the apples and slice into thin wedges. Use a sharp knife to split the vanilla bean in half, if using, and set aside. In a large skillet, melt the butter over medium-high heat. Add the light brown sugar, vanilla bean or vanilla extract, and lemon zest to the butter and mix until combined. Place the apples in the pan and allow them to simmer and brown evenly on both sides. When the apples reach a semisoft texture, remove them from the heat and set aside. Remove the vanilla beans and discard.

Simple Syrup

Everyone needs a simple syrup to count on—this is mine. Makes about ½ cup (150 g).

Ingredient	Metric	Weight	Volume
Granulated sugar	75 g	2.64 oz	heaping ⅓ cup
Water	75 g	2.64 oz	scant ½ cup
Lemon wedge*	1	1	1

*Use if storing the syrup for more than 1 day.

In a medium-size saucepan, combine the sugar and water. Bring to a boil and stir until sugar has dissolved. Allow to cool. Store covered in the refrigerator for up to 4 weeks.

Sliced Almond Crunch

Sugar-crusted almonds—a delicious topping for nut lovers. Makes about ¾ cup (110 g).

Ingredient	Metric	Weight	Volume
Sliced, blanched almonds	50 g	1.76 oz	½ cup
Granulated sugar	50 g	1.76 oz	¼ cup
Egg whites	10–20 g	0.35–0.70 oz	Up to ½ egg white

Combine the sliced almonds and granulated sugar in a bowl. Slowly add enough egg whites to create a sandlike texture.

Smoked Salmon Spread

Pairs great on bagels and English muffins—you can even try it on a biscuit! Makes about 1 cup (225 g).

Ingredient	Metric	Weight	Volume
Cream cheese, softened	225 g	8 oz	1 (8-oz [225 g] package
Smoked salmon	Up to 100 g	3 oz	1 yolk
Fresh dill or thyme	1 g	0.03 oz	1 tsp
Fresh ground pepper	To taste	To taste	To taste

*Any smoked fish can be substituted for the salmon.

Place the softened cream cheese into the mixing bowl of a stand mixer and use the paddle attachment to cream the cheese. Using a sharp knife, roughly chop the smoked salmon into small pieces. Mince the fresh thyme or dill to a fine consistency. Add the herbs and salmon to the cream cheese and mix with the paddle attachment until uniformly incorporated. Add fresh ground pepper to taste. Serve immediately or chill overnight.

Sugar glaze

Sticky Bun Smear

Melts into a sugary glaze when baked—yummy! Makes about 1 cup (284 g).

Ingredient	Metric	Weight	Volume
Unsalted butter, softened	112 g	3.95 oz	8 tbsp
Granulated sugar	60 g	2.11 oz	¼ cup
Light brown sugar	55 g	1.94 oz	¼ cup, packed
Honey	57 g	2 oz	3 tbsp

Bring the butter to room temperature and then cream together with the granulated and brown sugars until you achieve a light and creamy consistency. Slowly add the honey and continue to blend thoroughly. Place in a plastic container and keep in the refrigerator for up to 1 week.

Sugar Glaze

Mark this page! This tried-and-true glaze will become a favorite. Makes about 1 cup (195 g).

Ingredient	Metric	Weight	Volume
Vanilla bean (optional)	¼ bean	¼ bean	¼ bean
Whole milk	Up to 35 g	1.23 oz	Up to 2 tbsp
Light corn syrup	10 g	0.35 oz	1 tbsp
Powdered sugar	150 g	5.29 oz	1⅛ cups

Split the vanilla bean in half, if using, and scrape out the seeds with the point of a sharp knife. In a saucepan, combine the milk, corn syrup, and vanilla bean seeds, heat until 140°F (60°C), and then remove from the heat. Remove the vanilla bean. In a separate bowl, sift the powdered sugar, then add to the milk mixture, stirring with a whisk until a smooth consistency is achieved. Use immediately on warm product, or cover the surface with a plastic film and place in the refrigerator overnight to use the following day. Stir through before use and apply to the warm product.

Troubleshooting

Every baker, from the professional to those at home, wants to make the best impression with their recipes and formulas. The "perfect bake" is almost as elusive to a baker as a no-hitter is to a baseball pitcher in baseball: It is possible . . . when everything comes together perfectly under just the right conditions. It can happen, and when it does, there is nothing more satisfying!

However, in the real world of baking, we struggle to balance a multitude of variables, from temperatures to times to techniques. The following information will help you identify some common mistakes and teach you the changes necessary to ensure success.

Quick Breads

CREAMING BUTTER AND SUGAR

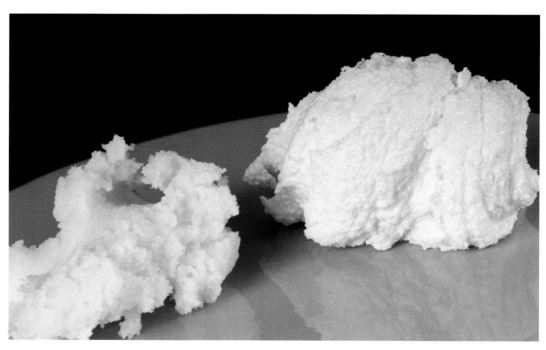

When combining butter and sugar in the creaming method, make sure that you mix them long enough to properly incorporate the air. Note: The butter should be at room temperature (70°F to 75°F [21° to 24°C]). The sample on the left has not been creamed long enough, whereas the sample on the right is a properly creamed butter and sugar mixture. Notice the lighter, fluffier texture and the lighter color due to the incorporated air. It is very difficult to overcream butter and sugar, so when in doubt, mix a little longer.

IMPROPER CREAMING

Proper temperature is the key to successfully incorporating eggs and a creamed butter mixture. Here is an example of what happens when the difference of temperature between the creamed butter and eggs is too great. Most often the eggs are too cold compared to the butter mixture. To remedy this, you can warm up the metal bowl over the flame of a gas range or use a propane torch (often used for making crème brûlée) while constantly stirring the mixture. To prevent this, the eggs and butter should both be at room temperature (70° to 75°F [21° to 24°C]) before they are incorporated.

MIXING QUICK BREADS

It's easy to overmix a quick bread batter. The batter in the foreground has been overmixed: the longer mixing time resulted in more air being incorporated and gave the batter a lighter color. The batter in the background has been properly mixed—until the ingredients just came together. Overmixing develops a stronger gluten structure than is desired in quick breads and results in tunneling (see page 160).

TUNNELING

Tunneling happens when a batter has been overmixed and the gluten developed to a point that it starts to trap larger pockets of air within the product. These pockets of air tunnels can be seen in the loaf on the left. The loaf on the right has been properly mixed. Notice that both loaves have a nicely shaped domed top, but the overmixed batter results in more volume through the excessive air that has been incorporated during the mixing process.

UNDERBAKED

An underbaked quick bread will have raw batter in the center or near the top of the product. Insert a cake tester or wooden skewer into the center of a quick bread to check for doneness—if it comes out clean with no raw batter residue, it is completely baked.

OVERBAKED

This quick bread was baked at too high a heat. Notice the thick, uniform, dark browning around all edges. Sometimes hot spots in an oven or an incorrectly calibrated oven is the cause. Baking at a lower heat for a longer period of time would solve this problem.

Pre-ferments

POOLISH

Whether a biga, poolish, or sponge, every pre-ferment goes through a fermentation cycle. The trick is to use it when it is as close as possible to its peak before it collapses. Here you see three stages of a poolish (from left to right): underdeveloped, ideally developed, and overdeveloped. Notice the bubbly surface and air cell structure in the ideally fermented poolish. The poolish on the right has gone beyond its peak and collapsed, leaving telltale "water mark" signs along the sides of the container.

BIGA

A biga is a stiffer pre-ferment with less water content; a fully developed biga will have a smoother top surface than a poolish and will have well-developed air cells. A biga will collapse in the center if overdeveloped.

Enriched Dough

UNDERDEVELOPED ENRICHED DOUGH

An underdeveloped enriched dough: Notice the shaggy texture of the dough.

OVERWORKED SHAPING

When shaping dough, take care not to overwork it. The round in the back is properly shaped; the outer dough membrane is silky and smooth and stretches nicely over the dried fruit and nuts incorporated into the particular formula shown. The round in the front has been overworked during the shaping process. Notice the ragged and unkempt surface texture—the result of tightening and tearing due to the buildup of too much strength during the overworked shaping.

GLUTEN DEVELOPMENT

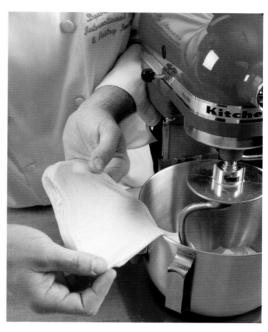

A gluten window test performed on an underdeveloped enriched dough: The gluten is not well developed and the dough tears when stretched.

A properly developed enriched dough after mixing: Notice the smooth, elastic texture of the dough.

Laminated Dough

CROSS SECTIONS OF TRIFOLDS

This photo illustrates the visual difference in laminated dough with a different number of trifolds: four trifolds (top), three trifolds (middle), and two trifolds (bottom). Ideal lamination is achieved when using three trifolds.

VARIATIONS IN BAKED TRIFOLDS

Laminated squares made from dough with a different number of trifolds: two trifolds (left), three trifolds (middle), and four trifolds (right). All squares were rolled to the same thickness, cut to the same size, and baked at the same temperature for the same amount of time.

CROSS SECTIONS OF BAKED TRIFOLDS

The cross sections of the same three laminated dough squares reveal the inner layers. When sampled by tasting, the two-trifold square will be heavy and have a gummy texture, the three-trifold will be soft and flaky, and the four-trifold will be tough and chewy.

CROSS SECTIONS OF CROISSANTS

Shown here are two cross sections of two different croissants: one made with two trifolds (left) and one made with three trifolds (right). Both were ideally proofed before baking. Notice that three trifolds result in better volume and more spider weblike connective layers. The croissant made with two trifolds has fewer layers and less volume.

PROOFING PROBLEMS IN CROISSANTS

Two cross sections of two croissants, both made with three trifolds. The croissant on the left was underproofed before baking, whereas the croissant on the right was properly proofed. Notice the difference in volumes; the dough at the center of the underproofed croissant never got warm enough to properly ferment and expand.

OVER-PROOFED CROISSANT

Pictured here is a croissant that has been proofed at a temperature greater than 82˚F (28˚C). Notice that the butter once contained in the laminated layers is leaking out of the croissant and pooling along the bottom edge of the dough. To avoid this, keep careful track of the ambient room temperature during proofing. When proofing croissants, a cooler room temperature results in a slower and longer proof, which yields a better performing and tasting product.

Charts and Conversions

METRIC & U.S. STANDARD WEIGHTS

1 gram	=	0.035 ounces
1 ounce	=	28.35 grams
1 pound	=	453.6 grams
1 kilogram	=	35.27 ounces

ARITHMETIC CONVERSIONS

To Convert	into	Multiply by
Grams	Ounces	0.035
Ounces	Grams	28.35

TEMPERATURE CONVERSIONS

Degrees in Celsius	x	1.8	+	32	=	Degrees in Fahrenheit	
Degrees in Fahrenheit	–	32	x	0.555	=	Degrees in Celsius	

YEAST CONVERSIONS

The formulas in this book were created with instant yeast. To convert the instant yeast amounts to either fresh yeast or active dry yeast, use the following conversion equations:

Grams (or ounces) of instant yeast	X	2.5	=	Grams (or ounces) of fresh (cake) yeast
Grams (or ounces) of instant yeast	X	1.25	=	Grams (or ounces) of active dry yeast

These conversions differ slightly from the manufacturers' recommended amounts. Artisan bread dough comes off the mixer at slightly cooler temperatures, and the general rule is to use just a bit more instant yeast than recommended.

Active dry yeast will need to be dissolved in warm water (100°F [38°C]) before being added to the dough. The change in temperature will cause the dough to ferment at a faster rate. Be mindful during fermentation or allow the water to cool to the temperature specified in the formulas.

BAKER'S PERCENTAGE

Professional bakers express many of their formulas in baker's percentage. Many serious home bakers have adopted this approach as well, because it allows a formula to be more easily increased or decreased as the desired yield requires. Each ingredient in the formula is expressed as a percentage of the total amount of flour in the formula (flour being the predominant ingredient). Flour's percentage is constant at 100 percent. If more than one type of flour is listed, the combination of the weights of all flours is 100 percent.

In the following hypothetical formula, the bread flour and whole wheat flour percentages add up to 100 percent.

Example:

Bread flour	800 g	=	80%
Whole wheat flour	200 g	=	20%
Water	650 g	=	65%
Salt	30 g	=	3%
Yeast	20 g	=	2%

Resources

Ingredients, Tools, and Equipment

Atlantic Spice Company
2 Shore Road
North Truro, MA 02652 USA
www.atlanticspice.com
Selection of gourmet spices, herbs, and tea

Bob's Red Mill Natural Foods
13521 SE Pheasant Court
Milwaukie, OR 97222 USA
www.bobsredmill.com
A leading resource in stone milling and a wide diversity of whole grains

Breadhitz
www.breadhitz.com
Tutorial DVDs on baking artisan and decorative breads; tools

Bridge Kitchenware
711 3rd Avenue
New York, NY 10017 USA
www.bridgekitchenware.com
Professional-grade bakeware and tools

C.H.I.P.S.
10777 Mazoch Road
Weimar, TX 78962 USA
www.chipsbooks.com
Great selection of books on baking, baking technology, and other culinary fields

Fantes
1006 South Ninth Street
Philadelphia, PA 19147-4798 USA
www.fantes.com
An extremely complete source of kitchenware

JB Prince
36 East 31st Street
New York, NY 10016 USA
www.jbprince.com
A great resource for culinary tools and equipment

King Arthur Flour
135 Route 5 South
Norwich, VT 05055 USA
www.kingarthurflour.com
A premier baking resource for flour, baking ingredients, tools, and education

Penzeys Spices
19300 West Janacek Court
Brookfield, WI 53045 USA
www.penzeys.com
A comprehensive offering of spices, seasonings, and herbs

Right On Scales
P.O. Box 710374
Santee, CA 92072-0374 USA
www.rightonscales.com
A comprehensive resource for digital scales

Sur La Table
www.surlatable.com
Bakeware, molds, and specialty tools, appliances, and books

Education and Organizations

Bread Bakers Guild of America

900 Fifth Avenue, 4th Floor

Pittsburgh, PA 15219 USA

www.bbga.org

The definitive resource for artisan bakers in the United States. Website includes extensive artisan bread–related links, including education

King Arthur Flour Baking Education Center

135 Route 5 South

Norwich, VT 05055 USA

www.kingarthurflour.com

Professional and enthusiast classes on bread and baking

Institute of Culinary Education

50 West 23rd Street

New York, NY 10010 USA

www.iceculinary.com

Founded by Peter Krump, this culinary school offers both career training and recreational courses

Johnson & Wales University

www.jwu.edu

Associate and bachelor degree programs in both Baking and Pastry and Culinary Arts; campuses located in Providence, RI; Charlotte, NC; Denver, CO; and Miami, FL

Notter School of Pastry Arts

8204 Crystal Clear Lane, Suite 1600

Orlando, FL 32809 USA

www.notterschool.com

Continuing education classes in baking and pastry; certificate diploma program

San Francisco Baking Institute

480 Grand Avenue

South San Francisco, CA 94080 USA

www.sfbi.com

Workshops and professional bread training program

Recommended Reading

Advanced Bread and Pastry: A Professional Approach by Michel Suas (Delmar Cengage Learning, 2008)

The Art & Soul of Baking by Sur la Table with Cindy Mushet (Kansas City: Andrews McMeel, 2008)

Art of Viennoiserie and Festival of Tarts by Joël Bellouet (France, 2004)

Artisan Baking Across America by Maggie Glezer (New York: Artisan, 2000)

Baking Artisan Bread: 10 Expert Formulas for Baking Better Bread at Home by Ciril Hitz (Beverly, MA: Quarry Books, 2008)

The Best Bread Ever by Charles Van Over (New York: Broadway Books, 1997)

A Blessing of Bread by Maggie Glezer (New York: Artisan, 2004)

Bread: A Baker's Book of Techniques and Recipes by Jeffrey Hamelman (Hoboken, NJ: Wiley & Sons, 2004)

The Bread Baker's Apprentice by Peter Reinhart (Berkeley: Ten Speed Press, 2001)

How Baking Works by Paula Figoni (Hoboken, NJ: Wiley & Sons, 2007)

Tartine by Elisabeth Prueitt and Chad Robertson (San Francisco: Chronicle Books, 2006)

The Taste of Bread by Raymond Calvel, translated by Ron Wirtz (Gaithersburg, MD: Aspen Publishers, 2001)

Whole Grain Breads: New Techniques, Extraordinary Flavor by Peter Reinhart (Berkeley: Ten Speed Press, 2007)

Glossary

baker's percentage: professional standard of calculating weight in a formula; the total flour weight is always considered 100 percent in comparison to the rest of the ingredients

biga: Italian-style pre-ferment with a hydration rate of 50 to 60 percent

blending: the process of mixing liquid fats and other wet ingredients with sugar.

bran: outer portion of the wheat kernel (or berry)

bulk fermentation: primary stage of fermentation

chemical leaveners: refers to leavening agents that break down to produce carbon dioxide gas (such as baking powder, baking soda)

creaming: the process of incorporating air into solid fats, usually with sugar

crumb: interior portion of the bread

elasticity: ability of a dough to spring back from pressure or manipulation; aided by the protein glutenin

endosperm: innermost portion of the wheat kernel from which most of the bread flour comes

enriched: refers to dough that has a high percentage of fat and sugar

extensibility: a dough's ability to be stretched or extended; aided by the protein gliadin

fermentation: process of yeast converting sugars into carbon dioxide; gives dough flavor and volume

germ: nucleus of the wheat berry where the next generation of the seed is stored

gliadin: protein in flour that gives extensibility; aids in forming gluten

glutenin: protein in flour that gives elasticity; aids in forming gluten

gluten: combinations of proteins that form a weblike matrix and capture gases, giving dough lift and structure

hydration: amount of liquids in a dough in relationship to the flour

hygroscopic: readily taking up and retaining moisture (for example, sugar is hygroscopic)

lamination: alternating layers of dough and butter that separate during the baking process

lean dough: a dough that contains no additional sugars or fats other than what is naturally present in flour

malt: substance derived from barley containing enzymes that are beneficial to the bread-baking process; referred to in bread baking as diastatic malt; can be either liquid or dry, used in the same weight ratio

old dough (pâte fermentée): pre-ferment that is kept from the original dough for an overnight cold fermentation and is added to the next day's dough

osmotolerant: form of instant yeast, designed to perform better in enriched doughs (such as brioche or croissant)

plastic: softened stage of butter that does not interfere with gluten development

poolish: 100 percent hydrated pre-ferment; favors a lactic flavor profile

pre-ferment: ingredients that are mixed and fermented before they are added to the final dough

preshaping: initial shaping that takes place to "train" the dough for its final shape

proofing: time the loaves are resting right after dividing or before baking

protein content: the percentage of gluten-forming proteins in a flour

quick breads: baked products that are chemically leavened, usually with baking soda or baking powder

room temperature: 70°F to 75°F (21° to 24°C)

rubbing: a mixing method that involves rubbing or cutting fat into flour

shaping: final forming of a loaf into the desired shape

simple syrup: sweet syrup made from water and sugar (1 to 1 ratio by weight)

sponge: pre-ferment that is hydrated at 60 to 63 percent; generally much wetter than the final dough to which it is added

transfer peel: long, thin board used to transfer the baguette from the couche to the peel

yeast: single-cell fungus used to ferment bread; takes sugars and transforms them into carbon dioxide and alcohol

Index

A

all-purpose flour, 18
apple kuchen, 108–109
apples, sautéed, 156

B

bagels, whole wheat cinnamon raisin, 96–97
baker's percentage, 167
baking forms, 37–38
baking powder, 27
baking soda, 26, 27
banana muffins, 86–87
Best Bread Ever, The (Van Over), 56
biga, 55, 161
biscuits, basic, 76–77
blending, 53
Bostock, 118–119
bran muffins, 90–91
brioche
   Bostock, 118–119
   classic, 100–101
   doughnuts, lemon, 102–103
   pumpkin cream, 104–105
   rum-raisin-almond, 106–107
brushes, pastry, 45
butter
   characteristics of, 22
   clarified, 113
   European vs. American-style, 22, 134
   seized, 52
butter block, making, 133–134
buttermilk, 73

C

carrot cake, 78–79
chocolate croissants, 144–145
chocolate muffins, 88–89
chocolate-cinnamon swirls, 146–147
cinnamon buns, 124–125
conversions, metric and standard, 167
conversions, temperature, 167

corn bread, 82–83
corn syrup, 20
cranberry-orange scones, 70–71
creaming, 52, 158–159
croissants
   basic, 140–141
   chocolate, 144–145
   proofing problems, 166
   three vs. two trifolds, 165
   whole wheat ham and cheese, 142–143
crumb topping, ginger, 73
cutters, circle and biscuit, 45

D

Danish, all-purpose, 136–139
dough, enriched
   defined, 99
   mixing, 56–58, 60–61
   optimum temperature for, 59
   proofing, 64
   recipes for, 100–129, 136–147
   retarding, 64
   shaping, 62–63
   troubleshooting, 161–166
dough, laminated
   defined, 64, 131
   pre-ferments, 54–55
   recipes for, 136–147
   set changes, frequent, 137
   techniques for, 132–135
   troubleshooting, 164–166
doughnuts, lemon brioche, 102–103

E

egg wash, 152
eggs
   freezing, 29
   functions of, 28–29
   separating, 28
English muffins, 45, 92–93
extracts, 30

F

fats, 21–23

fermentation, 25, 54

fillings

    almond paste, 150

    cinnamon bun, 151

    lemon cream, 152

    lemon curd, 153

    nut, 154

    pastry cream, 154

    pumpkin pastry cream, 155

    sautéed apples, 156

fiore di sicilia, 110

flavorings, compound, 31

flour

    milling, 16–17

    types of, 16, 17, 18, 129

food processors, 37

freeze, bake and, 65

friction factor, 59

G

gibassier, 115–117

ginger scones, 72–73

glazes

    Bostock syrup, 150

    chocolate, 151

    egg wash, 152

    lemon-almond, 152

    lemon-sugar glaze, 153

    sticky bun smear, 157

    sugar, 157

gluten, development of, 163

grater, box, 44

H

ham and cheese croissants, 142–143

herbs, 31

honey, 20

I

ice-cream scoops, 42

K

knives, 44

L

lamination. *See* dough, laminated

leaveners, 24–27

lemon brioche doughnuts, 102–103

lemon, zesting, 78

liqueurs, 31

M

malt, 121

margarine, 22

measuring

    conversions, 167

    equipment, 39

    guidelines, 48–49

microplane, 44

mixed-berry muffins, 94–95

mixers, 34–36

mixing

    bowls, 41

    enriched dough, 56–58, 60–61

    fruit, nuts, and seeds, 61

    fundamentals of, 56–58, 60–61, 159–160

    in food processor, 56

    temperature of dough, 59

muffins

    banana, 86–87

    bran, 90–91

    chocolate, 88–89

    English, 45, 92–93

    mixed-berry, 94–95

    pumpkin, 80–81

N

nut flours, 129

O

oils, 23
ovens, 36

P

panettone, 110–111
pans, sheet, 39
par-baking, 65
pastry wheels, 43
pâte fermentée, 55
pecan sticky buns, 122–123
poolish, 55, 161
pre-ferments, 54–55, 161
prescaling, 65
proofing, 64
proofing containers, 41
pumpkin cream brioche, 104–105
pumpkin muffins, 80–81
pumpkin, puree of, 81

Q

quick breads
   defined, 69
   recipes for, 70–97
   techniques for, 50–53
   troubleshooting, 158–160

R

racks, cooling, 42
retarding, 64
rings, English muffin, 45
rolling pins, 42
rubbing, 50–51
rum-raisin-almond brioche, 106–107
Russian braid, 128–129

S

salt, 30
savory scones, 74–75
scales, 34, 48

scones
   cranberry-orange, 70–71
   ginger, 72–73
   savory, 74–75
scrapers, 40
shaping, 62–63, 162
shortening, 22
sifters, 41
simple syrup, 156
spatulas, 43
spices, 31
sponge, 55
spreads
   almond Bostock paste, 150
   Butterkuchen paste, 150
   cinnamon bun filling, 151
   honey-nut butter, 153
   smoked salmon, 156
stollen, 112–114
strainers, 41
sugars, 18–20
sweet dough, basic, 120–121
sweeteners, 18, 20
syrups, 20, 150, 156

T

tea ring, 126–127
temperature, conversions of, 167
thermometers, 40
timers, 40
toppings
   cinnamon sugar, 151
   crumb, 73, 151
   crunch, 152
   sliced almond crunch, 156
trans fats, 23
trifolds
   different numbers of, 164–165
   making, 134–135
tunneling, 53, 159, 160

V

Van Over, Charlie, 56
vanilla, extract of, 30–31

W

weights, metric and standard conversions of, 167
wheels, pastry, 43
whole wheat flour, 17, 18

Y

yeast
    fermentation of, 19, 25, 54
    types of, 25–26, 167

Z

zucchini bread, 84–85

Acknowledgments

AS I WROTE THIS BOOK, I realized the book development process is akin to that of baking. You begin with an outline (or recipe) that contains the basic building blocks of information (or ingredients). They are combined in a certain order and mixed and kneaded and coaxed into shape, and with a bit of work and a little luck, the resulting whole is greater than the sum of the parts.

While I can hold my own in the bakeshop on most occasions, writing a book is a different story and there are many people to whom I owe thanks. These people were instrumental in the making (or baking) of this book and no matter what their role, their contributions shaped these pages on many levels.

To begin, there are countless people who have contributed to my development as an educator, a baker, and the person I am over the years—their names would fill many pages. You know who you are and I am indebted to you all.

To my friends and colleagues, Mitch Stamm and Richard Miscovich, for their intelligence, generosity, and wit.

To all of my colleagues at Johnson & Wales University, both faculty and administration, for their support over the years and for accepting, or at least tolerating, my crazy ways.

To my editor, Rochelle Bourgault, for her sensitive editing, comprehensive vision, and unflappable calm.

To the team at Quarry Books, including Betsy Gammons and David Martinell, for attending to critical details, many of which I am not even aware.

To Jennifer Brush, for her careful recipe testing and amazing attention to detail.

To the dedicated Johnson & Wales students who volunteered their time during photoshoots and helped out in many ways: Meryem Hail, Jesse Jackson III, Blake Lovelace, John Maieli, and Meaghan Tobin.

To all of my students, both past and present, whose constant questioning challenges me and keeps me on my toes, and to the bakers all over the world who continue to inspire me.

To Peter Reinhart, who planted the seed, and to Craig Ponsford and the Bread Bakers Guild of America, who gave me the opportunity to fly (and I don't just mean from coast to coast)!

To my children, Kira and Cailen, for their unconditional love and patience … the pool is calling!

And finally, to my wife, Kylee. This book would simply not exist without her.

About the Author

CIRIL HITZ is the Department Chair for the International Baking and Pastry Institute at Johnson & Wales University in Providence, Rhode Island. Ciril graduated from the Rhode Island School of Design, after which he returned to his native Switzerland and completed a three-year apprenticeship as a pastry chef/chocolatier. He received his first introduction to bread baking while in Europe, laying the foundation of skills that led him to where he is today.

Ciril has been recognized nationally and internationally with numerous awards and accomplishments. He was selected as a Top Ten Pastry Chef in America in both 2007 and 2008 by *Pastry Art & Design* magazine. In 2004 he competed in the National Bread and Pastry Team Championship, winning the overall team Gold Medal as well as all individual bread awards. He was a member of the Bread Bakers Guild Team USA that competed at the 2002 Coupe du Monde de la Boulangerie in Paris, France, where the team captured the Silver Medal. He has been a guest instructor and expert at many national and international culinary events and schools and serves on the advisory board of the Bread Bakers Guild of America.

Ciril is frequently seen on The Food Network and has been featured on the NBC *Today Show.* He is the author of *Baking Artisan Bread* (Quarry Books, 2008) and his work has graced the pages of numerous magazines and the interiors of exhibition halls and museums, including COPIA in Napa, California. He is the producer of his own line of educational DVDs and lives in Massachusetts with his wife, Kylee, and their two children. For more information on his work, visit www.breadhitz.com.

About the Photographer

KYLEE HUNNIBELL HITZ graduated from the Rhode Island School of Design with a BFA in industrial design and, after a short career in textile design, joined her husband in forming the company Breadhitz. With this book, she adds the genre of food photography to her experience in design and product photography. Kylee lives in Rehoboth, Massachusetts, with her husband and children and manages their busy life and business, as well as their mini-farm of chickens, pheasants, three cats, polar-bearlike dog, reclusive rabbit, and spunky Norwegian Fjord mare.